machine embroidery

machine embroidery

projects • techniques • motifs

Clare Carter

Photography by Linda Burgess

Quadrille

page 1: Button Collection (see page 62)
page 5: Pins with Panache (see page 82)

Illustrations · Kate Simunek

First published in 1996 by
Quadrille Publishing Limited
9 Irving Street, London WC2H 7AT

Published in association with the National Magazine Company Limited
Country Living is a trademark of the National Magazine Company Limited

Art Director · Mary Evans
Managing Editor · Jane O'Shea
Art Editor · Vanessa Courtier
Project Editor · Patsy North
Copy Editor · Sarah Widdicombe
Editorial Assistant · Katherine Seely

British Library Cataloguing-in-Publication Data
A catalogue record for this book is available
from the British Library.

ISBN 1 899988 80 7

Printed in Spain

contents

Introduction

Using a sewing machine to work decorative stitching effects is a wonderful way of embellishing fabric. The embroidered effect can be as simple as using a contrasting thread for topstitching, or as intricate as a fine tapestry with a multitude of precisely placed tiny stitches.

This book is designed to be a gentle introduction to machine embroidery: the informative first chapter reacquaints the reader with the sewing machine, offers a guide to fabrics, threads and useful sewing accessories, and includes a practical section on transferring and marking designs. The next chapter, which includes the first designs to stitch, uses the machine set up for normal sewing but introduces the idea of stitching for decoration rather than solely to join or finish a fabric edge. The third chapter is about free embroidery, in which the fabric is moved in any direction by hand rather than backwards or forwards by the machine. The progression of designs starts with those using simple lines of stitching, gradually builds up to solid areas of colour, introduces the idea of altering the stitch tension and culminates in the creation of a joyful figurative picture. The final chapter includes a section on lettering, explains how to use vanishing fabrics and finishes with further tension effects.

Each project or design in the book is supported by a techniques section which explains fully the embroidery methods used. This makes the projects easier to work, while at the same time giving readers the necessary skills to use the methods for their own designs. The final section of the book includes small outlines for practising free-stitching techniques, as well as some alternative designs, and alphabets.

This book is written for anyone with access to a sewing machine. The combination of desirable, clearly explained projects with easily accessible technical information and useful problem-solving sections should make machine embroidery just as approachable as other, more traditional, forms of needlework.

Getting started

Machine embroidery is both intriguing and frightening. Picking up a needle and thread to embroider by hand seems an easier step to decorative stitching than using a sewing machine, but both are creative needlecrafts and the great advantage of machine embroidery is that the machine forms the stitches, allowing the embroiderer to concentrate entirely on the design. Moreover, while bending over a whirring sewing machine is perhaps not quite as peaceful as stitching by hand, working a project in machine embroidery does become a fascinating and utterly absorbing process.

All the projects and techniques presented in this book can be worked on a simple zigzag-stitch machine – there is no need for an electronic or computerized model, so anyone with access to an electrically operated sewing machine can have a go. Apart from this, machine embroidery requires few other tools or accessories, and any well-stocked workbasket should provide all the basic equipment that is necessary.

sewing machines

The machine embroidery techniques and projects in this book are designed to be produced on a fairly basic sewing machine. The designs in the Set-stitch Decoration chapter could all, with a couple of minor changes, be stitched with a straight-stitch machine. For the designs in the Free Stitching and Decorative Effects chapters, a swing-needle (zigzag-stitch) machine is helpful, but not essential. Read through the information below to refamiliarize yourself with the sewing machine and its different parts, but do not think of it as a shopping list – the latest computerized machine may be very desirable, but it is not necessary in order to create any of the designs in this book.

Types of machine

An electrically operated sewing machine, which leaves both hands free to control the fabric, is essential for free embroidery. There are many different types on the market, offering a range of facilities within each price bracket.

• All modern machines have a swing-needle bar, which means that they can do zigzag as well as straight stitching.

• Semi-automatic and automatic machines will have a variety of utility stitches as well as zigzag. The stitching patterns may be altered manually by inserting a specific cam, or the cams may be built in and selected by switching a lever or a button.

• Electronic machines will offer a much higher degree of control over the moving parts within the machine, as the position of the needle relative to the movement of the teeth and speed of stitching are all precisely co-ordinated.

• Computerized machines offer a huge variety of pre-programmed stitch effects, and often have memory facilities which allow individual adjustments to be stored and repeated.

The two most important settings to check when considering a machine for free embroidery are those controlling the teeth movement and the tension of the stitches.

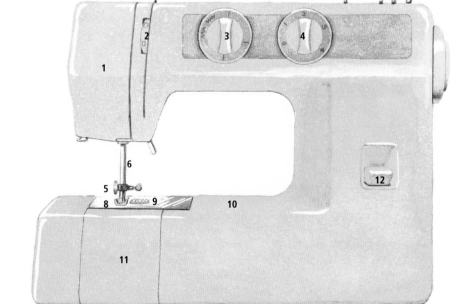

1   face plate
2   tension dial
3   width control/pattern selector
4   stitch-length selector
5   thumb screw
6   needle bar
7   thread guide
8   needle plate
9   teeth
10 bed plate
11 shuttle cover plate
12 reverse button

Teeth

When a machine is set for normal stitching, the teeth (feed dogs) automatically feed the fabric under the needle. For free stitching or embroidery the fabric must be moved by hand, so you will need to be able to disconnect or immobilize the teeth movement (see page 44). Most swing-needle machines will offer a darning or embroidery option, and this will include some facility for lowering or covering the teeth.

Tension settings

Some machine manuals advise against altering the tension, but it does no harm to the machine and minor adjustments are often necessary to achieve perfect stitching even when set stitching. When free stitching, more adjustments may be required or desired. It is possible to alter the tension on a machine with universal tension, but do refer to the manual, and note the original settings to be reset after stitching a particular effect.

top thread

bobbin thread

fig 1

fig 2

fig 3

Setting the tension

To check the tension for either set or free stitching, thread the top and bobbin with contrasting colours of thread and stitch a few lines of straight stitching.
• If top and bobbin tensions are correctly set, no contrasting thread will appear on either side of the fabric (fig 1).
• If the bobbin thread is appearing on the top surface of the fabric (fig 2), first loosen the top tension, stitch and check again. If the thread is still appearing, tighten the bobbin tension and stitch again. Continue to loosen or tighten until a perfect stitch is achieved.
• If the top thread is being pulled to the underside of the fabric (fig 3), first tighten the top tension, check by stitching, then loosen the bobbin tension and recheck. Continue adjusting to create a perfect tension, and note the tension settings before adjusting to create unusual effects.

Top tension It is easier to alter the top tension, so always start by adjusting here. On most machines, the top tension is set by moving a dial on which the higher numbers represent the tighter tensions – normal tension for set stitching is usually between 3 and 5. Some machines will simply have + or – signs, with normal in the middle.

Bobbin tension Your machine may have either a vertical bobbin case or a horizontal bobbin case, which is often fixed in the shuttle race.
• On a vertical bobbin case, the tension is adjusted by a small tension screw (fig 4). There may also be a larger screw which holds the case together. If there are no + or – signs, turn the tension screw clockwise to tighten tension and anti-clockwise to loosen it. It is very easy to unscrew the screw completely and lose it, so work over a piece of soft cloth which will catch the screw if it drops.
• A built-in horizontal bobbin case will usually have a tension screw facing upwards underneath the needle plate (fig 5). Many will have a numbered scale or + and – signs; if not, note the angle of the screw head before adjusting.

fig 4

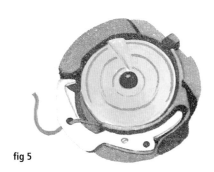

fig 5

Needles

Machine embroidery requires sharp, strong needles. If a needle is having trouble stitching through thick or heavily worked fabric, move up a size.

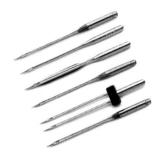

Needles are sold in a combination of English/US and Continental sizes:

English/US
8 9 10 11 12 14 16 18 20
Continental
60 65 70 75 80 90 100 110 120

There are various types of needle.
Standard needle Choose a heavier needle for embroidery than for seaming.
Ballpoint needle Useful for stitching synthetic fabrics or if the machine is skipping stitches.

Jeans needle Tapered and with a very sharp point, useful for embroidering on tough fabrics.
Topstitch needle Larger eye will take a heavier thread or wool.
Twin needle Available in a variety of sizes sold with a double figure, for example 3/80. The first is millimetres between needles, the second the actual needle size. Makes narrow double lines of stitching which can be used for spaghetti quilting (see page 35).
Wing needle Spear-shaped head leaves a distinctive hole on the right fabric.

Machine feet

Free machine embroidery is often stitched without a foot, or with a darning foot if preferred, but the feet listed below are common attachments that are useful for decorative stitching.

Presser foot Basic foot suitable for straight and zigzag stitching.
Open-toe presser foot Choose a transparent plastic one to offer the maximum view of decorative set stitching.
Embroidery foot Wide space underneath allows for a build-up of decorative embroidery stitches and the grooves underneath make stitching curves much easier.
Darning foot Usually spring loaded, allowing it to bounce over uneven embroidered surfaces.

Pintuck foot Useful for working even rows of twin-needle pintucks.
Tailor-tacking foot Stitches loops which can be used for faggoting or fringes.
Zipper foot Can be moved to left or right of the needle, allowing stitching to run very close to the teeth of a zip or other raised surface. A central needle position, used for straight stitch only, is useful for quilting.
Cording foot Useful for couching work, a hole in the front of the foot ensures cord is fed into the correct position to be stitched over.

darning foot

zipper foot

cording foot

open-toe presser foot

pintuck foot

Machine maintenance

Specific machine-care tips are given for the various embroidery techniques throughout the book, but a little time spent on general maintenance of your machine will greatly enhance its performance.

• Do clean your machine regularly; using it for embroidery means that it will be stitching for longer periods, and machine embroidery threads are softer than sewing threads and create more fluff and lint, so regular brushing and declogging of the shuttle race and all mechanical parts is essential.

• Refer to your sewing-machine manual for oiling instructions. Older machines need to be oiled frequently, but some newer ones are self lubricating and applying oil to them might affect their performance adversely. Use only sewing-machine oil, and after oiling do stitch on waste cloth for a minute or so to ensure that no excess oil is going to seep out on to the fabric.

• When using the machine for free embroidery projects, work in 20-minute spells or less to prevent the machine engine overheating.

fabrics & threads

There are no set rules to machine embroidery. It does not require special canvas or evenweave fabric, and designs can be worked with ordinary sewing threads or with special embroidery threads. The guidelines below are intended to help new embroiderers, or to suggest alternatives or solutions if the fabric or threads that have been tried are not producing a satisfactory effect.

Fabrics

Fabrics which have an even weave, in which the threads are regularly spaced and cross at right angles, will be the easiest to embroider, as they have the same amount of give in both directions and can easily be stretched tightly in an embroidery hoop. However it should possible to embroider on almost any fabric by following the tips below.

For set-stitch decoration

If machine embroidery is being used to decorate the fabric but not to obscure it, as in set-stitch decoration, the fabric should be chosen purely for its decorative qualities and practical application to the finished purpose. The embroidered decoration is worked using set-stitching techniques – that is, with the machine set up for normal stitching – so the decorative stitching should pose no extra problems.

For free embroidery

Fabrics which are to be stitched using a free machine-embroidery technique must be stretched tight in an embroidery hoop to provide a firm base for stitching (see pages 16 and 50).

Free-stitching techniques vary greatly. If the stitching is to cover only a little of the fabric surface, the fabric must be chosen for its looks and purpose and, as long as it is a firmly woven fabric which can be stretched tightly in a hoop, it will be possible to embroider it. On the other hand, if the fabric is to be completely covered with embroidery, it will be the foundation for a great many stitches and must be strong. Choose an evenly woven cloth made from natural fibre – calico is ideal.

Natural fibres tend to be stronger than synthetics and will separate to allow the needle through. Silk is an ideal fabric for free stitching as it comes in a wealth of colours, weights and finishes, can be stretched tightly in a hoop and is stronger even than cotton.

With a synthetic fabric, the needle is more likely to cut a hole through the fibres. These, and shiny fabrics, are more difficult to stitch than others, but the stitching problems can usually be overcome by using new, sharp needles or a ballpoint needle.

Very fine or sheer fabrics such as organza can be used in a double layer, laid over or even bonded to a stronger, natural-coloured base fabric. Lightweight fabrics can be backed with a stabilizer (see opposite).

Try tacking stretch fabrics to calico with numerous rows of cross-tacking, before mounting in a hoop. Stitching on stretch fabrics can create an attractive smocked effect.

For free stitching with a foot

The same considerations as for free embroidery apply to free stitching with an embroidery or darning foot, the only difference being that because the foot holds the fabric firmly for the needle to enter, it does not need to be stretched as tightly as for free stitching.

If the fabric is firm, or backed with interfacing or some sort of stabilizer (see opposite), it should be possible to hold it by hand rather than mounting it in a hoop. Read through the different techniques detailed on pages 44–45 and 50–51, and decide which method is most suitable for your chosen fabric.

Lining and backing

Using a lining, interfacing or other backing fabric will alter the working quality of a fabric, making it possible to embroider otherwise difficult fabrics and changing the character of some fabrics to give quite different stitching effects. Any firmly woven fabric may be used as a backing, but there is also a whole range of specialist fabrics that can be very useful.

Wadding

Polyester wadding is available in light, medium and heavy weights, all of which are suitable to use for incorporating into a machine stitched project. The medium weight is probably most suitable for quilting, as it will give a pleasant raised effect to the quilted areas but will also remain flexible and therefore drape well. Wool and cotton waddings are also available, which are warmer but give a flatter, less textured appearance to the finished quilt.

Interfacing

Interfacing is available in light, medium and heavy weights.
• Fusible interfacing has an adhesive side which will adhere firmly to the fabric when ironed; it forms a very good bond and a firm foundation for stitching, but also alters the character of the fabric, making it much less pliable.
• Non-fusible interfacing is more suitable for adding body without altering the appearance of the fabric. The fabric is pinned or tacked securely over the interfacing and the two layers are then treated as one when being stitched.
• Pelmet interfacing is particularly firm and, although easy to stitch through, will create a stiff effect (see the Decorated Box on pages 46–49).

Bonding web

Double-sided fusible interfacing, or bonding web, will fix one fabric to another, and is ideal for appliqué projects or for creating layers of sheer fabrics with stitching details between them (see the Table Settings on pages 94–96). A fusible hemming tape is also available, useful for bonding the folded-under edges of a stitched picture.

Stabilizer

A stabilizer is a non-woven material similar to interfacing which is used under a fine fabric to give it sufficient body for decorative stitching. Some types are pinned or tacked in place, others are slightly adhesive. After embroidering, the stabilizer can be torn away easily from around the stitching.

Vanishing fabric

Vanishing fabrics were developed to create a surface on which to work machine embroidery. Lines of stitches are worked to form an interconnecting net, which can then be embroidered further to create either a lacy or a densely woven effect. When stitching is complete, the vanishing fabric is dissolved away by various methods. For guidance on using vanishing fabrics, see pages 80–81.

Threads

The main difference between sewing and embroidery threads lies in their thickness and strength. Mercerized sewing thread is twisted tightly and then treated chemically to make it stronger, which is necessary for seaming but not for decoration. Embroidery threads are finer, which means that there is much more on a reel and when working blocks of colour the fibres spread out to create a denser mass.

Both types of thread offer a range of colours, but many more variegated and metallic effects are available in embroidery thread. Machine embroidery threads are available in a wide variety of natural and synthetic fibres with a choice of matt or lustre finishes. Threads with a blend of fibres are stronger.

15

hoops & other equipment

Apart from a sewing machine, the only other essential piece of equipment for machine embroidery, particularly free embroidery, is an embroidery hoop or frame. These are widely available from haberdashery and craft shops, but since they are also used for hand embroidery, you may already have one. Similarly, you will probably already possess many of the other items listed here as part of your general sewing equipment.

Embroidery hoops

Embroidery hoops and frames may be made from plastic, wood or metal and are available in a range of sizes. They are usually circular but may also be rectangular.

For most machine-embroidery purposes you should choose a circular wooden hoop with a fixing screw to tighten it, as this type will hold the fabric most securely. The hoop should be somewhere between 12cm (5in) and 20cm (8in) in diameter and no more than 6mm (¼in) thick, so that it can slide easily under the machine needle. If a wooden hoop is thicker, saw a small cut part-way through one side through which to slide the needle.

A spring-loaded plastic hoop can be useful for working on very lightweight fabrics which tear easily, as it will not grip the fabric so tightly.

Binding a hoop

If a wooden hoop is not holding the fabric taut, or the fabric is slipping during stitching, the grip can be improved by binding the inner hoop with a cotton twill tape or gluing narrow velvet ribbon around the outside of the inner hoop.

To bind with tape, secure one end of the tape to the inner hoop using a spot of all-purpose glue. Bind the tape diagonally around the hoop, stretching it tightly while wrapping and overlapping the preceding edge at each turn. Fix the end with another spot of glue and allow to dry before using.

To bind with velvet ribbon, choose a ribbon which is no wider than the hoop. Follow the instructions above, gluing a single layer of ribbon around the outside of the inner hoop and butting the ends together neatly. Allow the glue to dry completely before using.

Mounting fabric in a hoop

1 Place the outer hoop on a clean, flat surface and then lay the fabric right side up over the hoop, making sure that the design is centred.
2 Press the inner hoop into the outer one and gently pull the fabric all round to make a taut drum.
3 Push down the inner ring firmly so that the fabric is held quite flat against the surface and tighten the fixing screw. The inner ring should protrude slightly below the outer ring to hold fabric correctly.

General equipment

To make up any of the projects in the book or, indeed, to experiment with the different stitching techniques, it would be useful to have the following equipment or accessories readily available for each embroidery session.

Scissors
Use large dressmaker's scissors for cutting fabric, household scissors for cutting paper patterns, and small, sharp scissors for trimming threads, unpicking and for cutting out threads jammed in the shuttle race.

Seam ripper or unpicker
Useful for slashing through layered fabrics, cutting through loops of satin stitching to create fringed effects and for unpicking misplaced stitches.

Tape measure
A tape measure or long ruler is essential for measuring fabric quantities.

Pins
Sharp dressmaker's pins are essential for most projects.

Hand-sewing needles
Most of the projects in the book require some hand finishing, so a selection of these, including a darning needle and a bodkin, is useful.

Needlecase
Keep all your needles in a needlecase, including any machine needles reserved for particular threads (see page 23). Hand stitch a length of the relevant thread next to each needle's position for reference if you wish.

Bobbins
It is very useful to have extra bobbins, so that each thread is instantly available without having to wind one colour over another or throw away thread to make a bobbin available. Store bobbins in a divided bobbin box, so that they are visible and remain neatly wound.

Bobbin case
If your work frequently uses altered bobbin tension techniques (see pages 92–93) and you use a machine with a vertical bobbin case (see page 11), it is useful to have one bobbin case permanently set to a normal tension and a second bobbin case set to a loose tension. Mark one of the bobbin cases with a spot of nail varnish to distinguish them easily.

Needle guard
If the correct hand position is used on a hoop or to grip the fabric, it is very unlikely that the needle will come into contact with your hand. However, this is a common worry and some machine manufacturers produce a clear plastic needle guard as an accessory.

Pencils and markers
Most projects will require an outline to be marked on to the fabric before stitching. Use either a very sharp, hard pencil or a specialist marker (see page 18).

Other drawing tools
A straight-edged ruler, a pair of compasses and a set square are useful for accurate marking out on fabric.

preparation & aftercare

Whether you use the patterns and designs in this book, find outlines from other sources or draw your own sketches on paper, you will need to transfer the lines on to the fabric before stitching. To make most of the projects in this book the outlines will need to be enlarged before transferring, and this may apply to other artwork as well. Finally, the finished embroidery may have become unacceptably distorted and will need to be stretched back into shape.

Enlarging

Most of the design outlines in this book cannot be shown actual size because of space limitations. Similarly, designs taken from other sources may need to be scaled up or down before they are stitched.

The simplest method of enlarging a design is to use a photocopier. The design outlines in this book that require enlarging each have the correct percentage enlargement noted beside them. For other designs you might wish to embroider, work out the required finished size (height and width), take it with the design to a photocopy shop and ask for help in working out the percentage.

Marking and transferring

For all but the simplest lines of decorative stitching, you will need to transfer the outlines of a design on to the fabric before stitching. Your choice of marker will be influenced by the stitching – will the stitches be worked in fine lines, as on the Decorated Box on pages 46–49, or will they cover the background and hide all the lines, as in the Lying on a Rug picture on pages 66–69. Consider also whether the finished article will need to be washed or not. Whatever marker you choose, try it out on a waste scrap of fabric first to see how obvious it is, whether it smudges and whether it will be possible to remove it if necessary.

Markers

• For lines which may not be hidden completely by the stitching, use a very sharp, hard pencil and make the lines as fine as possible.

• Alternatively, use a water-soluble marking pen or a vanishing pen, available from needlecraft shops and haberdashery departments; these make lines that can be removed.

Water-soluble pen marks disappear when sprayed with water, but make sure your fabric and threads are colourfast. Vanishing pens work very well on some fabrics and not on others. The line should fade after two or three days, but

sometimes the line appears to fade and then reappears some days later!

For both types of marking pen, do not iron the fabric while the lines are still visible, as this will fix them permanently.

• Tailor's chalk is the traditional marker and, if it has a sharp edge, makes a good removable line for quick stitching, but it would wear off if used to draw the outlines of an intricate design.

• Lines which will eventually be hidden can be marked in pencil, or with an indelible, fine felt-tipped pen if a more obvious line is preferred.

• For marking lines on vanishing fabric, use an indelible, fine felt-tipped pen.

Transferring methods

There are several different methods of transferring a machine embroidery design from paper to fabric.

• Lay the fabric over the outline, place both on a light box and simply trace off the lines. A similar technique is to pin the fabric over the outline and tape both to a large window pane.

• Place a piece of dressmaker's carbon paper (tracing paper) over the fabric, with the design outline on top of that, and then draw over the outline using a sharp pencil.

• Use the old-fashioned method of tracing the outline, turning the tracing paper over and drawing over the lines using a sharp, soft pencil. Then lay the tracing right way up on the fabric and draw over the lines again. The outline should have been transferred on to the fabric and can be redefined using a hard pencil or permanent felt-tipped pen.

• Alternatively, draw on the back of the tracing using a special transfer pencil, then apply the image to the fabric by pressing with a warm iron.

• For simple shapes, such as the roof pieces of the Decorated Box on pages 46–49, or the circles in the Button Collection on pages 62–63, or for a motif that will be used repeatedly, cut out the shape from card and use this as a template.

Aftercare

Both hand and machine embroidering frequently tend to distort the shape of the fabric. An uneven surface may add to the character of the design, but if a wavy outline or undulating surface detracts from the finished effect, the embroidery can be pressed or stretched to reduce the distortion.

fig 1

Pressing

Before pressing a machine-embroidered piece, consider carefully whether it is really necessary. If the fabric has been pressed before stretching in a hoop, the embroidered area should not need pressing afterwards.

Pieces stitched with ordinary mercerized sewing thread will respond well to pressing, and most machine embroidery threads will withstand quite hot temperatures – except the metallic ones, which should be pressed with a cool iron and caution – but pressing any embroidery obviously flattens the stitches, and this can detract from the finished effect.

If you need to press an embroidered piece and are anxious not to flatten the stitches, lay the embroidery right side down on a bath towel and press the back of the work lightly using a steam iron, avoiding any downward pressure on the iron.

Stretching

To stretch a piece of embroidery, you will need some fibre or block board at least 1cm (⅜in) thick and larger than the finished design, a similar-sized old blanket or towel, an ironing or plant water spray and rustproof drawing pins.

1 Lay the blanket or towel over the board and dampen it by spraying.

2 Lay the embroidery on top and spray lightly with water. Most thread and fabric colours will be colourfast with a light spray, but check the fastness of any hand-dyed threads or fabrics.

3 Secure the embroidery to the board in the centre of each side with a drawing pin, stretching it slightly.

4 Working on alternate sides and away from each central pin, stretch and pin the sides until the pins meet at the corners and the embroidery is flat (fig 1).

5 Leave until thoroughly dry and then unpin. Do not try to speed up drying by placing the work near direct heat.

Set-stitch decoration

The simplest piece of topstitching along a seam or a satin-stitch edging on a pillowcase qualifies as machine embroidery. Whereas the techniques for embroidering or embellishing by hand are quite different to those used for stitching an item together, exactly the same machine-stitching techniques can be used for utility or decorative work.

Creating an ornamental effect by machine can be as simple as stitching a single line. For your first forays into machine embroidery, as illustrated by the projects in this chapter, there is no need to adjust the machine settings – a whole variety of attractive effects can be achieved simply by threading up and starting to stitch. The decoration is created by choosing effective combinations of thread colours, experimenting with those little-used attachments provided with most machines, pressing and pleating the fabric, or by quilting it subtly to create softly padded relief patterns.

getting started

Using a sewing machine for embroidery need not entail learning any new techniques or skills – just working lines of contrasting coloured stitching across a piece of plain fabric can be all the decoration that is required to transform a simple design into a decorative piece. Stitching embellishment on to the fabric in this way, rather than using the machine for seaming pieces together, is also a useful introduction to working on all parts of a piece of fabric rather than just around the edges.

Setting up the machine

The four projects in this chapter all require the sewing machine to be set up for normal set stitching. If the machine is unfamiliar to you, consult the manual for advice on inserting the bobbin, how to thread and other general instructions, but even if the machine is one you have used a lot for general sewing, it is worth spending some time cleaning and adjusting it to achieve the best possible performance for embroidery (see Problem solving opposite).

Starting to stitch

It is always a good idea to work some sample stitching on scraps of spare fabric, but when the stitching is to form the decoration it is even more important to work a test piece first, using the fabric, interfacing or wadding and threads that are to be used for the actual piece.

Always hold the threads out of the way at the start of stitching so that they do not knot or tangle, and get used to finishing stitching with the thread take-up lever at the highest point or just past it, so that when stitching is recommenced the top thread is not pulled out of the needle.

Start and finish every line of stitching with a few straight stitches in reverse to secure.

Straight stitch

1 Sew a few lines of straight stitch and remove the test piece from the machine.
2 First check that the tension is correctly adjusted (see page 11); if necessary, use a different-coloured top thread for further test stitching so that tension faults are more obvious.
3 Then consider the stitch length: setting 3 is average, but finer fabrics will need a lower setting and heavy fabrics a higher one. The length chosen should glide across the work without causing it to pucker. As a general guide, on lightweight fabrics choose a slightly shorter stitch setting for decorative stitching than for seaming.

Zigzag and satin stitch

Satin stitch is simply zigzag stitch worked with a very short stitch-length setting, so that the stitches are so close together that they form a solid bar. All machines have a variety of stitch-width settings.

Any tension problems will be much more obvious with zigzag or satin stitch and may cause pinching or puckering of the fabric. If the bobbin thread is appearing on the top side (below left), loosen the top tension slightly. If the top thread is being pulled under (below right), tighten the top tension. With perfect tension, the threads are drawn equally into the fabric. For instructions on adjusting tension, see page 11.

Decorative techniques

The methods of stitching are no different to those used for ordinary sewing, but as the stitching is intended as decoration it will be more visible. To enhance the decorative effect, try backing the fabric with interfacing (see page 15) which will quilt the fabric slightly, creating a sharpened, raised effect.

From the top: short straight stitch, triple stitch, zigzag stitch, satin stitch, satin stitch ribbon, a utility stitch pattern

Open corner   Closed corner

Straight-stitch effects

• For a small piece of work, such as the silk bags on pages 24–27, a short stitch length (with the tension properly adjusted) will create a slightly raised line of stitching – working such short stitches on a larger piece could be tedious!

• When straight stitching small grids, try using the reverse button or setting for alternate lines of stitching.

• Some machines have a triple-stitch facility, which works three stitches at every stitch position. A similar effect can be achieved by stitching carefully over a line of stitching so that the needle enters the original holes.

• To create defined corners, always pivot stitching lines with the needle through the fabric. Remember to raise the presser bar before pivoting and lower it before recommencing stitching.

• For narrow parallel lines, stitch with one side of the machine foot alongside the first row of stitching. To achieve wider parallel lines, use a quilting bar or measuring arm as a guide; this screws into the back of the foot (see your sewing machine manual) and can be adjusted so that one end rests on the previous line of stitching.

Zigzag and other stitch effects

• Experiment with different length and width settings for zigzag and satin stitch.

• Practise satin stitching to achieve the closest setting possible. Start with 1 and gradually reduce it: too close and the machine will begin to make some stitches over others, creating an uneven finished effect.

• Alter the width setting while the machine is stitching satin stitch, to create graduated ribbons of stitching.

• Loosen the top tension very slightly for satin stitch embroidery, to create a rounded bar effect rather than flat stitching.

• When making zigzag or satin-stitch corners, the position of the needle is important. If it is at the inside point of the corner when the fabric is pivoted, the result will be an open corner. If it is at the outside point, the corner will be closed and more angular.

• Practise stitching satin-stitch curves with an embroidery foot. To stitch perfect circles, draw them around a template or using a compass and stitch carefully over the lines. Alternatively, try taping a drawing pin to the needle plate, with the point through the tape. Push the fabric on to the pin and stitch – the fabric will automatically be fed in a circle. Changing the position of the pin will change the circle size.

• Try out any other utility stitch patterns the machine can produce, such as shell stitch, blind stitch or scallops.

Problem solving

• Damaged needles are the most common cause of skipped stitches or poor stitching. A bent needle may hit and nick the needle plate, which could then tear or pull on the fabric, so check needles frequently.

• Every thread wears a different groove in a new needle, and using one needle for different threads may cause thread breakages. If you have experienced this problem, try keeping a needle for each type of thread used.

• Clean your sewing machine regularly, brushing out any fluff from the teeth and shuttle race and around the needle bar.

• An unevenly wound bobbin may cause irregular stitching. If the loaded bobbin does not resemble a neat reel, refer to your manual for how to adjust the mechanism.

bags of style

Three silk bags enhanced with lines of stitching show just how simple it is to develop utility stitching into a decorative effect. The embellishment on the bags is created with combinations of straight, blind and satin stitches, often using a measuring arm, quilting bar or the side of the foot to work parallel lines of stitching to form different grid effects. Choose a limited range of thread colours, including repeats of the fabric shades.

   The bags illustrated are self lined with silk to use as evening bags or jewellery pouches, but the two larger ones could also be lined with shower-curtain fabric to make deliciously decadent yet practical washbags.

Stitch methods
Set straight stitch
Set satin stitch
Set blind stitch
Tension: normal settings throughout

Feet: normal presser foot, plus
   measuring arm or quilter foot with
   quilting bar, if available
Needle: 12/80

Ring bag

You will need
2 pieces silk dupion, each 20 x 30cm
   (8 x 12in), in contrasting colours
20 x 30cm (8 x 12in) sew-in medium-
   weight interfacing
Sewing thread in 2 contrasting colours
Sewing thread to match lining
1m (1¼yd) cord
Eyelet punch and eyelets (optional)

To prepare the fabric
1 Enlarge pattern piece to 156% and then to 156% on a photocopier and add a 1cm (⅜in) seam allowance all around.
2 Cut out 2 bag pieces from each colour

of silk and lay aside the 2 lining pieces. Cut out 2 bag pieces from interfacing. Press all pieces.
3 Back each bag piece to be embroidered with an interfacing piece, pinning or tacking layers together.

To work the embroidery
Work decorative lines of stitching to cut edges when appropriate, securing at each end. Back of bag has a simple grid with short bars of satin-stitch detail; front has horizontal lines of straight stitch and a satin-stitch cross in centre of bag, with circles of stitching radiating around it.

To make up
1 Lay each embroidered bag piece right sides together with a lining piece and stitch all round with a 1cm (⅜in) seam allowance, leaving a small gap to turn through. Trim, turn right side out and hand stitch gap closed. Press.
2 At narrowest part of neck, mark 2 eyelet holes on each bag piece as indicated on pattern piece. Either use an eyelet punch to secure an eyelet in each, or work small buttonholes.
3 Lay embroidered sides of bag pieces together, and stitch circular body parts together with a 3mm (⅛in) seam allowance. Turn bag right side out and press. Thread cord twice around bag through eyelets or buttonholes.

Enlarge to 156% and then to 156% on a photocopier and add 1cm (⅜in) seam allowance all around.

Enlarge to the measurements shown and add a
1cm (⅜in) seam allowance all around.

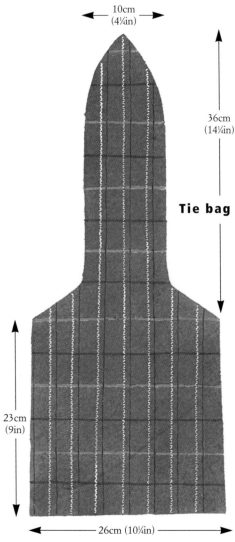

Tie bag

10cm
(4¼in)

36cm
(14¼in)

23cm
(9in)

26cm (10¼in)

26

You will need
2 pieces silk dupion, each 65 x 60cm
(25½ x 24in), in contrasting colours
65 x 60cm (25½ x 24in) sew-in medium-
weight interfacing
Sewing thread in 2 matching and
2 contrasting colours

To prepare the fabric
1 Enlarge pattern piece on the left to the
measurements shown.
2 Cut out 2 bag pieces from each colour
of silk and lay aside one of each colour
to use for lining when making up. Cut
out 2 bag pieces from medium-weight
interfacing. Press all pieces.
3 Back each bag piece to be
embroidered with an interfacing piece,
pinning or tacking layers together
securely so they do not slip.

To work the embroidery
Work a stitched grid over each bag
piece, using the photograph above as a
guide for the grid. Use matching sewing
thread colours for satin stitch lines and
contrasting sewing thread colours for
utility or zigzag lines.

To make up
1 Lay each embroidered bag piece right
sides together with a contrasting lining
piece and stitch all round with a 1cm
(⅜in) seam allowance, leaving a small
gap to turn through. Trim, turn right side
out and hand stitch gap closed. Press.
2 Lay embroidered sides of bag pieces
together, and stitch sides and base
together with a 6mm (¼in) seam
allowance, finishing securely at both
ends. Turn bag right side out and press.

Rectangular bag

You will need

66 x 49cm (26 x 19¼in) silk dupion
Contrasting silk dupion scraps
66 x 49cm (26 x 19¼in) sew-in medium-
    weight interfacing
10 x 30cm (4 x 12in) bonding web
Sewing thread in 2 matching and
    2 contrasting colours
2m (2¼yd) cord
Eyelet punch and eyelets (optional)

To prepare the fabric

1 Press rectangular silk and interfacing pieces and then back silk piece with interfacing, tacking layers together.
2 Back scraps of contrasting silk with bonding web following manufacturer's instructions, and cut out 13 triangles using template below.
3 Lay triangles along one short edge of rectangle as shown in fig 1, with triangle bases approximately 4cm (1½in) from rectangle edge and outside points of end triangles approximately 2cm (¾in) from rectangle sides. Iron triangles in place.

To work the embroidery

Work a simple linear grid of straight stitch, zigzag stitch and satin stitch over rectangle, as shown in photograph on page 26. Continue lengthways stitching lines across lining half, but work shorter, widthways stitching lines and satin-stitch bars on outer, appliquéd half only. Continue all lines of stitching to cut edges and secure at both ends.

To make up

1 With right sides together, fold embroidered rectangle in half widthways and stitch together around cut edges with a 1cm (⅜in) seam allowance, leaving a small gap to turn through. Trim, turn right side out and hand stitch gap closed.
2 Measure 5cm (2in) down from folded edge and mark 8 evenly spaced eyelet points for cord. Either use an eyelet punch to secure an eyelet in each, or work small buttonholes.
3 With right sides together, fold bag in half widthways and stitch side and base together with a 6mm (¼in) seam allowance. Turn bag right side out and press. Thread cord twice around bag through eyelets or buttonholes (fig 2).

triangle template

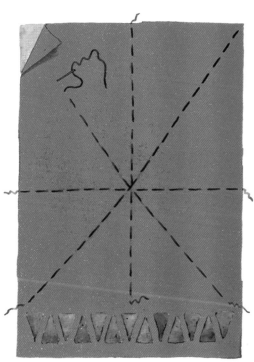

fig 1

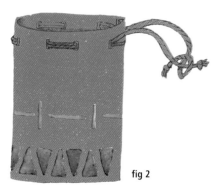

fig 2

27

unusual feet & needles

Even the oldest treadle sewing machine was supplied complete with a box of specialized feet and attachments. Modern machines have a whole variety of attachments and programs designed to make home sewing easier and more professional, but although the wide range of applications might have been an important selling point, once home they can easily be forgotten. So, spend some time sorting out the attachments to your machine, and then stitch some samples to remind yourself of their decorative potential.

Tailor-tacking foot

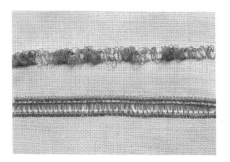

The tailor-tacking foot (see page 12) has a raised bar in the centre and is used with zigzag stitch. The top tension is loosened slightly to allow each top stitch to form into a loop.

This foot can be used to form fringes or to make a line of faggoting. For a fringe, set the stitch length to 1 or less and the width as wide as possible, and work a line of satin stitch. It can be left as a looped fringe or trimmed.

The stitches are not secured into the fabric, so they must be fixed in some way. Either iron a strip of iron-on interfacing to the wrong side or, when the line of fringing has been stitched, replace the normal presser foot, retighten the tension and, holding the fringing to one side with your finger, work a row of narrow satin stitch over the base of the loops.

Faggoting

Faggoting is a method of joining two pieces of fabric with a delicate line of stitches and holes, and is often seen as hand-worked embroidery on old linen towels and pillowcases.

1 Lay two pieces of fabric right sides together, with the cut edges neatened and lying even, and stitch the seam with a 6mm (¼ in) seam allowance (fig 1).
2 Gently pull the layers of fabric apart and press the seam allowances open (fig 2). Replace the normal presser foot, retighten the tension and stitch along the folded fabric edge on either side of the faggoting with a narrow satin stitch.

Alternative faggoting techniques

It is possible to work faggoting without a tailor-tacking foot on a machine with a faggoting stitch or a 3-step zigzag utility pattern.
1 Trim the seam allowances to 6mm (¼ in) and neaten, then press to the wrong side to make crisp, folded edges.
2 Tack one folded edge to a strip of tear-away stabilizer. Measure exactly 3mm (⅛ in) across the stabilizer and tack the second folded edge in place.
3 Centre the machine foot over the gap and stitch along it, ensuring that alternate edges are caught in the stitching. Tear away the stabilizer.

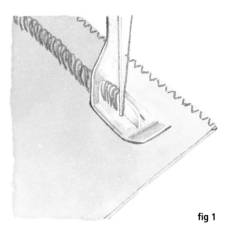

fig 1

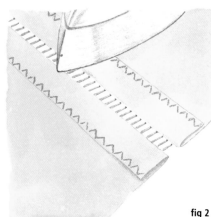

fig 2

Twin needles

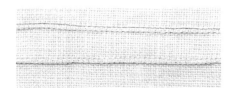

The effect of twin-needle stitching is to create slightly raised pintucks, which are much finer than pleated pintucks. Most swing-needle machines can be fitted with a twin needle for straight stitching, while some can also use one on a narrow zigzag setting of up to 2, but no wider or the needle will hit the needle plate. There are a variety of sizes of twin needle available (see page 12), and they can be used with a normal presser foot or with a grooved pintuck foot, which is useful for sewing exactly parallel rows of fine pintucks.

• Follow the instructions in the manual for threading your machine for twin-needle stitching. The threads are initially threaded together but are separated at the tension disk or lowest thread guide.

A single bobbin thread is used.
• The rows of pintucks created by twin-needle stitching can be worked in a self colour for a subtle effect or with 2 slightly different shades of thread.

Wing needle

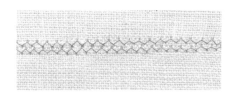

Wing needles are used to replicate traditional hand hemstitching, in which threads are drawn out of linen handkerchiefs or bedlinen and the resulting holes embellished with hand stitching. Wing needles work by pushing the threads apart to form a hole. They are available in standard needle sizes and also as twin needles, which actually have one wing needle with a standard needle on the same shank.

• A successful result with wing-needle stitching depends largely on the choice of fabric. Crisp, natural fabrics work best: the fabric must have a loose enough weave for the wing needle to push the threads apart rather than cutting or pulling them, and it must be firm enough to retain the hole once the needle has been withdrawn.

• Prepare fabrics for wing needle stitching by spraying with spray starch and pressing them well.
• Experiment with stitching more than once into the holes to increase the effect, or try zigzag (using a single wing needle only). Alternatively, tighten the top tension slightly to increase the size of the holes created.

Problem solving

• For a successful result when working zigzag stitching with a twin needle, it may help to loosen the bobbin tension slightly (see page 11).

• Using an open-toe presser foot rather than a normal presser foot makes it easier to see what is happening when working a decorative stitch effect.

crib cover

Log-cabin quilting, with a central square surrounded by increasingly long strips of fabric, has an American name but is also a traditional British patchwork method. It is an ideal way to use up old household linen and to try out a variety of stitches and new techniques.

Look out for old-fashioned tea towels, damask tablelinen, linen sheets, huckaback towels and any other washable fabrics of a similar weight. Work sampler centre squares of all the decorative stitch patterns your machine produces, then trawl through the attachment box and try out the tailor-tacking foot and any other little-used devices. Surround the squares with strips, and then either stitch them into a delightful baby's crib cover or make them up into a bolster, cushion cover or cottage curtain.

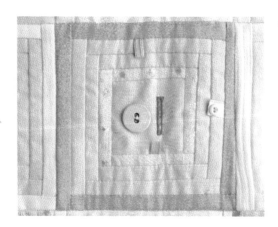

Stitch methods
Set straight stitch
Set satin stitch
Set utility stitches
Tension: normal settings throughout
Feet: normal presser foot, open-toe presser foot, tailor-tacking foot
Needles: 12/80; wing needle, twin needle (optional)

You will need
For a crib cover measuring 84 x 60cm (33 x 24in):
1.5m (1¾yd) in total of assorted lightweight fabrics, 90cm (36in) or 112cm (44in) wide
70 x 100cm (28 x 39in) warm backing fabric
3m (3½yd) satin ribbon, 4cm (1½in) wide
Sewing threads in assorted colours, for decoration
White sewing thread, for making up
Assorted linen buttons, cotton tape, name tapes, lace and ribbon
Rotary cutter and board (optional)

To cut out

1 Each finished log-cabin block measures 12cm (4¾in) square. For each square, you will need to cut out a 5.5cm (2⅛in) central square and long strips of fabric, each 2cm (⅞in) wide. These must be accurate, so that finished blocks are all exactly the same size. Using pencil and ruler, mark cutting lines lightly on wrong side of fabric.

2 Using rotary cutter and board (the most efficient method of cutting a number of layers accurately), for crib cover cut out 35 central squares and a mass of strips. Each block requires approximately 2m (2¼yd) of strips, which can be any length from 5.5cm (2⅛in) to full width of fabric.

To embroider the central squares

Use central squares to try out effects of different stitching patterns: straight stitch, different widths of zigzag and satin stitch, and any utility or decorative stitch pattern available on your machine. Make buttonholes on some, and use a button attachment to sew on old linen buttons. (**NB** Buttons on a baby's crib quilt should be attached *very* securely.)

Try faggoting with a tailor-tacking foot, or experiment with a wing needle on a crisp linen square. Other squares could have ribbons or rows of tape laid across them. (**NB** Again, on a baby's quilt ensure that they are stitched down adequately.) Some damask or huckaback squares can be left plain.

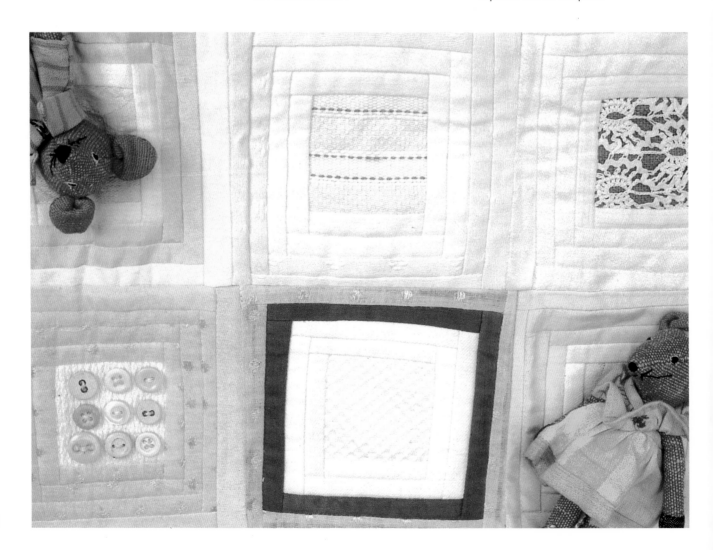

To work a log-cabin block

1 Lay a central square and a fabric strip right sides together, with one end of fabric strip level with edge of square (fig 1). Cut other end of strip level with opposite edge of square. Stitch square to strip with a 5mm (¼in) seam allowance, securing at both ends (it is vital that you use accurate seam allowances). Press seam open.

2 Turn square through 90° and apply a second strip of same fabric as before (fig 2). Press seam open.

3 Turn square as before and apply a third strip in same manner, then repeat once more so that central square is completely enclosed (fig 3).

4 Using either same or different fabric, repeat steps 1–3 to enclose square again. Continue to add fabric strips until each side of central square has 4 strips stitched around it.

fig 1

fig 2

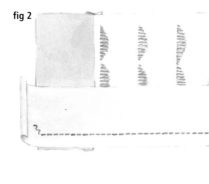

fig 3

To make up

1 Make up 35 blocks, trim any which are slightly big or uneven and lay out to form a pleasing design 5 squares wide by 7 squares long.

2 Sew first row of 7 squares together with 5mm (¼in) seam allowances. Repeat for remaining 4 rows of 7 squares. Press all seams open, join rows together and press seams open.

3 Trim backing fabric to same size as patchwork, place wrong sides together and pin all round. Lay right side of satin ribbon along one edge of patchwork with edges even, and stitch with a 1cm (⅜ in) seam allowance. At corners, create a diagonal tuck to make a mitre (fig 4). Fold end of ribbon under at join.

4 Fold ribbon to underside of cover and slipstitch edge down by hand.

fig 4

pleating & quilting

Machine embroidery is often used to apply surface decoration to a piece of fabric, but there are a whole variety of attractive effects to be created by altering the character of the fabric through padding or pleating. Lines of stitching can be used to form the fabric into crisp tucks or pleats, softly quilted layers or neat channels. The choice of thread colour will determine whether the stitching is a discreet part of the overall effect or a distinctive embellishment.

Pleating

A variety of effects can be created by pleating and stitching, from the subtle lines of twin-needle pintucks to deep furrows of folded fabric. Once the initial pleating is complete, it can be topstitched or formed into waves by cross stitching. To form precise pleats, spend time on the preparation, measuring and marking out carefully, and the actual stitching will be simple to work.

Plain pleats

Pleating uses a surprising amount of fabric: allow 2½–3 times the finished length, or calculate the fabric quantities accurately. It may help to draw out the pleating pattern on plain or graph paper.
1 Work out the depth of pleats required, taking into consideration the weight of the fabric – a thick fabric will be too bulky for fine pleats – then decide on the distance between them (placement area). When working out the fabric quantity err on the generous side, as all the folding and stitching tends to reduce both the width and the expected length.
2 Cut out a rectangle of fabric, ensuring that the corners are square, and lay it right side up on a clean, hard surface. Using a long ruler and sharp, very hard pencil, draw a line across the width of the fabric a short way from the edge and parallel to it. Using a set square against the ruler for accuracy, measure the pleat's finished width down from the first line and draw a parallel line, then repeat: when folded along the centre one, these three lines will form the first pleat. Measure the placement area width from the last line and draw another block of three lines. Continue to measure and mark to the other end of the fabric (fig 1).
3 Thread your sewing machine with matching thread at top and bobbin, and

set to straight stitch and a 2.5 to 3 stitch length. Fold and press the first pleat, then stitch directly along the marked line to secure it. Continue to fold, press and stitch the pleats in the same way to the end of the fabric.

Cross-stitched pleats

1 Measure along the completed plain pleats and divide the fabric into even sections, adding a generous trimming allowance at each side.
2 Using a quilting bar or measuring arm (see page 23) to ensure straight lines, stitch across the pleats from alternate marked points.
3 Turn the fabric through 180°, and stitch straight lines back across the pleats half-way between each original line of stitching, ensuring that the pleats lie in opposite directions to create a wave effect (fig 2).

Contrast topstitching

1 Before cross stitching the pleats, thread your machine with contrasting thread at top and bobbin and test the tension on a fabric scrap: it should be as near perfect as possible (see page 11).
2 Stitch three evenly spaced rows along the length of each pleat, making sure that the same colour is always on top.
3 Replace the contrasting thread with the self colour before cross stitching.

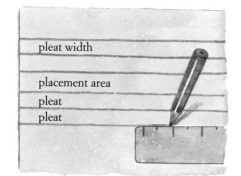

pleat width

placement area

pleat

pleat

fig 1

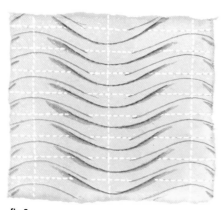

fig 2

Quilting

All sorts of quilting effects can be created quickly by machine. Spaghetti, or Italian, quilting is stitched first and filled afterwards. Another effect, similar to trapunto, or stuffed, work can be created easily using wadding and machine stitching.

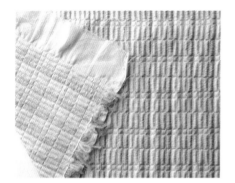

Spaghetti quilting

Spaghetti quilting is formed by stitching narrow channels on a transparent silk fabric and then threading double knitting or coarse embroidery yarn through them. It is a delightful effect, which can be enhanced by using coloured wools that create softly muted shades when seen through the lightweight silk, and by stitching the channels with a twin needle.

Choose a very fine, white or ivory transparent silk, and the same quantity of white muslin. Allow about 5cm (2in) extra on each side, as the technique will reduce the fabric area.

1 Lay the silk right side up over the muslin and, starting in the centre, tack the layers together (fig 3). Using tailor's chalk and a ruler, draw a line across the top of the fabric parallel to the edge.

2 Set up the machine up for twin-needle stitching (see page 29) and stitch over the chalk line. Using the outside of the foot as a width guide, stitch a second line parallel to the first (fig 4). Continue until all the fabric is stitched into evenly spaced channels.

3 Thread a blunt darning needle with two lengths of tapestry yarn used double and, working from the muslin side, thread it into a channel and work the needle along to the end. Thread all the channels with yarn in the same way.

The wool colours will change considerably when seen through the silk, so take the fabric with you to hold over the yarn when choosing shades.

Trapunto quilting

True trapunto quilting, or stuffed work, is formed by laying one fabric over a backing fabric, stitching outline shapes to form contained areas, and then cutting through the backing fabric and stuffing each outline separately. Alternatively, it can be worked by placing stuffing under appliqué patches and sewing them on to the fabric.

A similar effect, which is better suited to machine embroidery, can be created using a printed fabric with a pattern composed of fairly bold outline shapes.

1 Make a quilting sandwich of backing fabric (right side down), wadding, and top fabric (right side up), and pin the layers together.

2 Starting in the middle, tack the layers together (see fig 3 left). It is important that the layers are not able to move independently of each other, or the finished effect may be marred by tucks stitched on the underside. On a large piece of work, you may also need to tack lines parallel to the edges of the fabric.

3 Set your machine for straight stitch, with a stitch length of about 3. Choose top threads to match the areas of the printed design, and use a bobbin thread to match the backing fabric throughout. Stitch around some motifs, working the amount of quilting to suit the fabric design – a neat repeating pattern will be enhanced by regular quilting, while a more abstract design can be quilted in a fairly random manner.

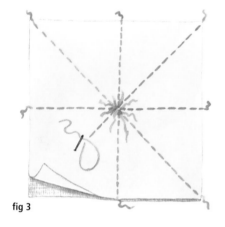

fig 3

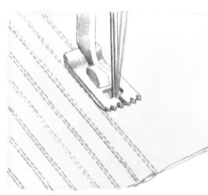

fig 4

pleated & pressed cushions

A combination of natural colours and precisely stitched pleats and channels creates a collection of cushions which are simply satisfying. A limited number of fabrics and colours were chosen, and these are combined to make individually attractive cushions that also work together as a pleasing group. The decorative stitching could not be simpler – on each cushion the effect is created by parallel lines of straight stitching, the secret of success being to measure and mark out the stitching lines accurately and to stitch precisely, so that all the pleats or channels are exactly the same width.

Spaghetti-quilted cushion

Stitch methods
Set straight stitch
Tension: normal settings throughout
Feet: normal presser foot, zipper foot
Needles: 1.6/70 twin needle, 12/80
    ordinary needle

You will need
For a cushion 40cm (16in) square:
50cm (20in) square transparent silk
50cm (20in) square muslin
43 x 90cm (17 x 36in) backing fabric
Ivory sewing thread
12 10m (11yd) skeins tapestry yarn
    (3 skeins each of 4 colours)
1.8m (2yd) fine piping cord
30cm (12in) zip
40cm (16in) square cushion pad
Blunt darning needle

To work spaghetti quilting
1 Following instructions on page 35, lay transparent silk square over muslin square and tack together. Using tailor's chalk, draw a fine line across centre of square. Thread machine with ivory sewing thread and, using a twin needle, stitch along marked line. Using machine foot as a width guide, cover square with

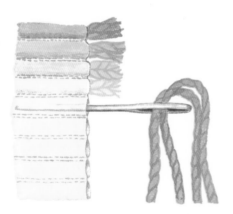

fig 1

equally spaced narrow channels.
2 Remove all tacking threads. Thread darning needle with 2 96cm (38in) lengths of tapestry yarn used double to create 4 strands, and work needle though first channel. Cut off yarn. Using 4 yarn colours in rotation, thread all channels in the same way (fig 1).
3 Using tailor's chalk, mark stitching lines at right angles to channels. Using normal single needle, stitch parallel lines of stitching across spaghetti quilting.

To trim the quilted square
1 Trim quilted square and backing fabric to 43cm (17in) square.
2 Cut extra backing fabric into bias strips 4cm (1½in) wide. Join to form a continuous strip 1.8m (2yd) long and use to cover piping cord. Trim cut edges to a 12mm (½in) seam allowance.
3 Pin piping all round quilted square. Stitch along stitching line on piping, using a zipper foot.

To make up
Make up cushion cover, leaving a 12mm (½in) seam allowance and inserting zip along one side. Insert pad.

Natural pleated cushion

Stitch methods

Set straight stitch
Tension: normal settings throughout
Feet: normal presser foot, zipper foot
Needle: 12/80

You will need

For a cushion 45cm (18in) square:
71 x 79cm (28 x 31in) rough silk
Light and dark contrasting sewing
    threads
2m (2¼yd) fringed edging
35cm (14in) zip
45cm (18in) square cushion pad

To cut out

Follow cutting layout in fig 1 and cut
1 cushion back, 2 short front panels and
1 long front panel to be pleated.

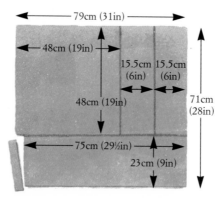

fig 1

To work the pleated panel

1 Press long front panel and, using a
ruler and set square, draw a pencil line
1cm (⅜in) from and parallel to one 23cm
(9in) edge. Follow instructions for
pressing and stitching plain pleats on
page 34, forming pleats 5mm (¼in) wide
and 2cm (¾in) apart (fig 2).
2 Topstitch each pleat with 3 lines of
stitching, using a dark thread in needle
and a contrasting light thread in bobbin
(see page 34).
3 Measure 1.5cm (½in) in from a side
edge and, following instructions for
pressing and stitching plain pleats on
page 34, stitch 3 parallel lines, each
10cm (4in) apart, in opposite directions,
to create a decorative wave effect (fig 3).

To make up

1 Trim pleated panel to measure 48cm
(19in) long. With right sides together,
stitch a plain front panel to each long
side of pleated panel just inside lines of
stitching which hold pleats in place.
2 Trim pleated square to same size as
back square. Leaving a 12mm (½in)
seam allowance all around, make up
cushion cover, incorporating fringed
edging and inserting zip along one side.
Then insert pad.

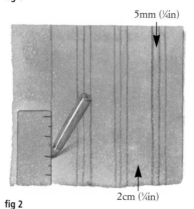

fig 2

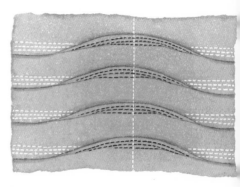

fig 3

Cream pleated cushion

Stitch methods
Set straight stitch
Tension: normal settings throughout
Feet: normal presser foot, zipper foot
Needle: 12/80

You will need
For a cushion 45cm (18in) square:
23 x 51cm (9 x 20½ in) fine silk
48 x 96cm (19 x 38in) rough silk, plus
    50 x 96cm (20 x 38in) extra for bias
    strips
Matching sewing thread
3m (3¼ yd) fine piping cord
35cm (14in zip)
45cm (18in) square cushion pad

To work the pleated panel
1 Press fine silk rectangle and, using a ruler and set square, draw a pencil line 1.5cm (½ in) from and parallel to one 23cm (9in) edge. Follow instructions for pressing and stitching plain pleats on page 34, forming pleats 1cm (⅜ in) wide and 1.5cm (½ in) apart, to make a panel 23cm (9in) square.
2 Measure 1.5cm (½ in) in from a side edge and, again following instructions on page 34, stitch parallel lines each 5cm (2in) apart in opposite directions to create a wave effect.

To trim the pleated panel
1 Cut out 2 48cm (19in) squares from rough silk.
2 Cut extra fabric into bias strips 4cm (1½ in) wide. Join to form a continuous strip 3m (3¼ yd) long and use to cover piping cord.
3 Pin a length of piping all around pleated square. Stitch close to cord, using a zipper foot. Trim seam allowances and fold underneath, so that piping surrounds panel.

To make up
1 Lay piped panel centrally on a rough silk square. Pin and slip stitch carefully in place, with stitches hidden under piping.
2 Stitch remaining piping around outside of cushion front, leaving a 1.5cm (½ in) seam allowance.
3 Using other square of rough silk for cushion back, make up cover, leaving a 1.5cm (½ in) seam allowance and inserting zip along one side. Insert pad.

summer, winter bedspread

Quilting a bedspread by hand is a labour of love – quilting by machine is a much quicker and more feasible prospect. Our seasonal bedspread is made as two quilts which can be used singly on summer nights and then buttoned together to form a warm winter cover. Either choose a bold printed design for the top side of the upper quilt to provide shapes to quilt around, or turn to pages 98–99 for some alternative quilting outlines. The under quilt is simply stitched with straight lines, forming a grid.

fig 1

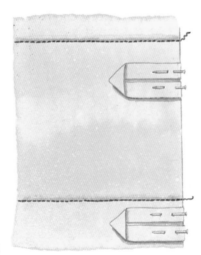

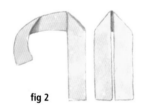

fig 2

Stitch methods

Set straight stitch

Tension: normal settings throughout

Feet: embroidery or quilting foot, normal presser foot

Needle: 14/90

You will need

For a finished bedspread 226 x 135cm (89 x 54in):

226cm (89in) bold floral fabric, 135cm (54in) wide

3 pieces calico, each 226 x 135cm (89 x 54in)

2 pieces medium-weight polyester wadding, each 226 x 135cm (89 x 54in)

4 large reels sewing thread, in colours to match floral printing

1 large reel calico-coloured sewing thread

1 large reel contrasting sewing thread, for under quilt

7.5m (8½yd) bias binding, 3.5cm (1½in) wide, for each quilt

3.9m (4½yd) cotton tape, 2.5cm (1in) wide

26 buttons

NB When quilting near the centre of a quilt, roll up one side so that it fits more easily under the sewing-machine arm.

To make the upper quilt

1 Following instructions on page 35 (Trapunto quilting), make a quilting sandwich of floral fabric, wadding and calico. Pin and tack layers together.

2 Select flowers to be quilted and mark with a pin, tailor's tack or masking tape.

3 Fit embroidery or quilting foot to machine and thread bobbin with calico-coloured thread. Quilt around flowers, odd petals, stalks and leaves, using top thread colour appropriate to each outline.

4 Trim any uneven edges. Unfold one side of bias binding. Lay against floral fabric, right sides together and cut edges even, and pin or tack around entire edge. At corners, create a small diagonal tuck (fig 1). Where binding ends meet, lay one inside the other and fold cut end of outer one to inside to form a neat join.

5 Using normal presser foot, stitch binding to quilt. Fold unstitched edge of binding to other side and slip stitch to calico to cover stitching line.

6 Spacing evenly, sew buttons around quilt edges on top side.

To make the under quilt

1 Following instructions on page 35, make a sandwich of calico, wadding and calico. Pin and tack layers together.

2 On calico, lightly mark an irregular grid of stitching lines from about 7cm (2¾in) to 15cm (6in) apart, using a sharp, hard pencil or vanishing pen. Fit embroidery or quilting foot to machine and thread top and bobbin with a colour chosen from floral fabric (or use contrasting threads at top and bobbin). Stitch all lines in both directions and trim any uneven edges.

3 Cut tape into 26 15cm (6in) lengths. Fold each strip in half, open out and refold as shown in fig 2. Press all folds.

4 Lay under quilt over upper quilt and mark all button positions.

5 Lay folded tapes at marked positions on side of quilt to lie against bed, with cut edges of tapes and quilt even (fig 3).

6 Bind quilt edges following steps 4 and 5 for upper quilt, and then button quilts together to form a warm bedspread.

fig 3

Free stitching

Free stitching in its most advanced form involves working without a machine foot and manually moving the fabric in any direction to form stitches. It can be viewed either as the really creative part of machine embroidery or absolutely terrifying! Like riding a bicycle, free stitching is a technique which once learnt is never forgotten, but as the wheels wobble underneath you, or the first faltering free stitches are formed, it may seem unlikely that either skill is obtainable or even desirable. However, do try it: even a few free stitches can create a delightful effect. The skill needed can be acquired with a little practice and will open up a completely new range of stitching possibilities.

Beginning to free stitch should be seen as a progression from machine darning. Indeed, the first techniques described in this chapter are stitched with a darning foot with the machine teeth disengaged. Once you have achieved free stitching with a darning foot, try without – one method may feel more natural to you than the other.

free machine embroidery

Learning to use a sewing machine for free stitching is entirely a matter of confidence and practice. Both can be built up slowly – there is no need to choose a heavily worked design as a first project, or to start free stitching without using a foot. Most free-stitching designs can, in fact, be worked with or without the use of a foot, and there are advantages and disadvantages to each.

Some simple outlines and designs are given on pages 100–101 which are ideal for practising free stitching. First experiments may have to be consigned to the wastebasket, but any interesting effects – whether planned or accidental – should be kept, along with a note of how they were achieved. Other successful attempts can be mounted together to form a sampler, or can be made into greetings cards.

Setting up the machine

There is very little difference in setting up the machine for set or free stitching. Threading is just the same; the only alteration necessary for free stitching is to adjust the teeth to allow the fabric to be moved freely by hand. Certain embroidery effects will require alterations to the zigzag width or the tension.

Teeth

In set stitching, the teeth (see page 11) feed the fabric under the needle in a regular fashion. In free stitching, the fabric is controlled by hand and may be moved in any direction, as well as from front to back or vice versa.

• First lower or cover the teeth. Most sewing machines, and particularly those with embroidery or darning facilities, will have retractable teeth.

• Some sewing machines with fixed teeth will have a cover which clips or screws over the needle plate.

• If your sewing machine has neither option, unscrew the needle plate and see if it is possible to remove the teeth temporarily, replacing the needle plate for stitching.

• As a last resort, tape a sheet of card or plastic (with a central hole for the needle to pass through) over the needle plate.

Stitch length

Stitch length should be set to 0. The length of the stitches is determined by moving the fabric manually.

Zigzag width

Zigzag width should usually be set to 0, although altering it can create all sorts of interesting textural effects, from blocks of colour to tiny beads and random stitch patterns (see page 60).

Tension

The tension may not need altering when moving from set to free stitching. If the stitching is not satisfactory, try loosening the top tension slightly. Altering either the top or bobbin tension to create unusual effects is a well-used technique in machine embroidery (see pages 61 and 92–93).

Top and bobbin threads

Choose the same type of thread for the top and bobbin for early experiments with free stitching – a stronger or heavier weight of thread will cause a weaker one to break. (For successful methods of using uneven threads to obtain special effects, see page 93).

Whether to use the same colour thread at top and bobbin is a matter of personal preference.

• Using the same colour will give a more intense hue, especially when working on fine fabrics.

• If the tension settings have not been adjusted perfectly, some bobbin thread may be drawn through and will show on the right side of the piece of fabric. This can be developed into a shading technique (see page 61), but if it is not intentional, using matching colours will disguise the problem.

• Using a single bobbin colour throughout is quicker.

Using a darning foot

Many sewing machines will have a darning foot supplied or can be fitted with a standard one; some will also have one or more free embroidery feet (see page 12).

A darning foot is usually made from clear plastic and has a spring mechanism, which enables it to bounce over uneven fabrics or areas of stitching but holds the fabric in place for the needle to enter. It should always be used when working on fabrics without an embroidery hoop.

Advantages
• For the inexperienced, the darning foot may offer more protection to fingers.
• For free-flowing designs, it may help the stitching to move across the fabric more freely.
• It is easier to stitch very stiff or heavily worked areas with a darning foot.

Disadvantages
• Even though the foot may be clear, it does restrict visibility of the immediate stitching area, making accurate detail stitching difficult.
• In textured or heavily worked areas, the darning foot may become caught under loops of thread.

Starting to stitch

When you begin free stitching using a darning foot, the only difference in the sewing machine is the absence of the teeth, and the only new technique to learn is moving the fabric in any direction you wish by hand.

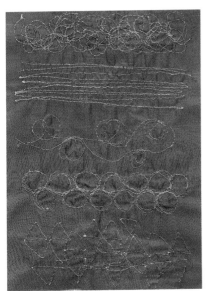

1 For first attempts, back each piece of fabric with a firm iron-on or sew-in interfacing (stitch the two layers together around the outer edges using set straight stitch), or experiment with tear-away stabilizers under the embroidery area (see page 15). Finer fabrics can always be stretched in a hoop when using a darning foot (see pages 50–51).

2 Hold the fabric flat against the machine bed, either by pressing your fingers on the needle plate on either side of the darning foot, or by holding the outer edges of the fabric but keeping your thumbs down so that the fabric is flat. Do not stretch the fabric, but ensure that the stitching area is taut.

3 Hold the threads to the back to avoid knotting and start to stitch. Secure the threads at the beginning by working a few stitches in the same hole or by reverse stitching a few stitches. Using a medium machine speed, move the fabric slowly – if you do not move the fabric manually it will remain stationary, and a knot will quickly form.

Concentrate on creating a line of stitches rather than one stitch at a time. Stitches can be any length, but begin by making them quite small (about the same as length 3 on set stitching). Tiny stitches are more difficult to make evenly and long ones tend to pull the needle and thread, causing either or both of them to break.

4 The stitches can be made in any direction, as well as backwards, sideways or in circles. Before attempting to work a particular design, experiment with straight lines worked in different directions, loops, S shapes, circles and repeating linear patterns (see pages 100–101). Practise stitching lines close together to create a block of colour, or stitching an outline and filling it in.

5 After working, pull all the threads to the back of the work, knot and trim.

Problem solving
• If the bobbin thread shows at each change of direction, loosen the top tension slightly.
• If the machine is skipping stitches, the fabric may be too loose. Hold it more tautly, stiffen it with a heavier weight of interfacing (see above) or stretch it in a hoop. Alternatively, the needle may be blunt or bent and should be changed.
• Move the fabric smoothly, as pulling or jerking will cause the needle to break.

45

decorated box

Making separate stiffened panels is an ideal way to practise free stitching. The stiffener creates a fabric firm enough to stitch over without an embroidery hoop, and the technique used employs a darning foot to give confidence to the nervous embroiderer!

Each panel is a sandwich of outer fabric, pelmet stiffener and lining fabric, held together with set straight stitch. Because some of the decorative stitching on the box is also part of the construction, the machine will need to be altered more than once from free to set stitching and back to free.

Choose fabrics and threads from the same palette of colours, so that each panel can be used as an individual sampler of stitch effects but, when joined together, they will form a delightful box.

Stitch methods

Set straight stitch
Set zigzag stitch
Free straight stitch
Couching with string
Tension: normal settings throughout
Feet: normal presser foot, darning foot
Needle: 14/90

You will need

For a box about 14cm (5½in) high:
10 x 71cm (4 x 28in) blue crêpe de chine
10 x 40cm (4 x 16in) purple crêpe de chine
10 x 50cm (4 x 20in) gold shot silk
10cm (4in) squares dark blue crêpe de chine, violet shot silk and red organza
10cm (4in) pelmet stiffener, 110cm (44in) wide
15cm (6in) square iron-on bonding web
Rayon machine embroidery thread:
  1 reel each burnt orange and charcoal
  2 reels indigo
  1 reel multicolour
1 reel gold metallic machine embroidery thread

64cm (25in) string dyed with blue ink
40cm (16in) undyed string
2 flat copper beads
8 small iridescent beads
Card for templates

To prepare the panels

1 From card, cut out a 9cm (3½in) square and a roof triangle using template on page 49. Use these templates to cut out 5 squares and 4 triangles from pelmet stiffener. Trim 3mm (⅛in) off each side of one square.

2 Use templates to cut out fabric squares and triangles, each 3mm (⅛in) larger all round than templates. Cut out 5 squares and 4 triangles from blue crêpe de chine, 4 squares from purple crêpe de chine, and 1 square and 4 triangles from gold shot silk.

3 Pin pelmet stiffener shapes between 2 fabric layers, to create a sandwich with fabric right side out on each side (fig 1). Stitch 4 large squares between blue and purple crêpe de chine, and smaller square and 4 triangles between blue crêpe de chine and gold shot silk.

fig 1

fig 2

To work the blue side panels

1 Work 2 side panels with blue crêpe de chine upwards. Thread top and bobbin with indigo thread, use a normal presser foot, and straight stitch up and down each panel in parallel lines.

2 Cut out 2 4cm (1½in) squares in gold shot silk and 2 in red organza. Lay organza on shot silk and pin centrally on each blue panel. Straight stitch in place, 6mm (¼in) from cut edges. Set stitch length to 1 and zigzag to 2.5, and stitch over straight-stitched line to form a solid satin-stitched square. Change top thread to multicolour, stitch length and zigzag to 3, and stitch over satin-stitched square (fig 2). Fray outer edges of small squares.

3 Using the photograph below left as a guide, mark positions of 4 corner spirals, suns and moons with a sharp pencil; draw a bird in 1 centre square and a tree in the other, using templates opposite. Change to darning foot and retract or cover teeth. Set to straight stitch and stitch spirals, using multicolour thread. Change top thread to gold for suns and moons. Change top thread to indigo and stitch bird and tree.

4 Trim rough edges of panels. Change to normal presser foot and lift or uncover teeth. Change top thread to charcoal, set stitch length to 1 and zigzag to 3½, and satin stitch around edge of each panel. Change top thread to multicolour, stitch length to 3 and zigzag to 4, and overstitch around each panel.

5 Hand sew an iridescent bead to each corner of central squares.

To work the purple side panels

1 Using normal presser foot and indigo top thread, straight stitch around outside of each square, with purple side up. Cut out 2 4cm (1½in) squares of blue crêpe de chine and 2 3.5cm (1¼in) squares of violet shot silk, and back each small square with iron-on bonding web. Lay small squares centrally over larger squares, and larger squares centrally on purple side panels, and iron in position.

2 Use photograph below right as a guide to stitch positions. Change top thread to gold and straight stitch a line on either side of central squares, using either a triple-stitch facility (see page 23) or, with stitch length at 3, stitching forward and back to form a thick line. Straight stitch twice around each central square.

3 Cut 4 10cm (4in) lengths of dyed string. Change top thread to multicolour, set stitch length and zigzag to 3, lay lengths of string across top and bottom of each panel and zigzag stitch over them. This technique is called 'couching' (see page 72).

4 Change to darning foot and retract or cover teeth. Set to straight stitch and stitch random spirals and scrolls around each central square. Change top thread to indigo and outline a diamond on each central square.

5 Using gold thread, hand sew a flat copper bead in centre of each square, creating a cross with stitching.

6 Finish outer edge of each panel, following instructions in step 4 for blue side panels.

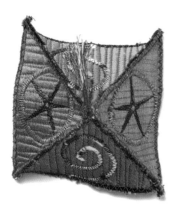

To work the roof

1 Stitch all roof panels gold side up, with longest edge of each triangle as base. Using normal presser foot and indigo top thread, straight stitch parallel lines up and down 2 panels. Change top thread to multicolour and straight stitch parallel lines on second pair of panels.

2 Change top thread to gold, stitch length to 1½ and zigzag to 3 and, using photograph on left as a placement guide, couch circles of dyed string on to 2 panels. Change top thread to indigo and, using varied stitch-length settings, couch spirals of undyed string on second pair of panels.

3 Using template below as a guide, draw a narrow, 5-pointed star in centre of each couched circle with a sharp pencil. Change to darning foot and retract or cover teeth. Change top thread to gold and set to straight stitch. Stitch outline of each star and then fill it in with a block of indigo stitching.

4 Trim rough edges of panels. Change to normal presser foot and lift or uncover teeth. Set stitch length to 1 and zigzag to 3½, and satin stitch around edge of panels, using indigo top thread on panels with spirals and burnt orange on panels with stars.

To assemble the box

1 With gold side of base square up, straight stitch parallel lines up and down square, using indigo top thread. Trim and neaten edges with satin stitch as for step 4 of blue side panels.

2 Change top and bobbin thread to burnt orange. With wrong sides together, lay a blue side panel on a purple one. Set stitch length and zigzag to 4 and join two side edges together. Repeat until all 4 sides are joined, making sure all sides are right way up.

3 Overstitch bottom of box to sides neatly by hand.

4 Machine stitch roof panels together, using charcoal top thread and burnt orange bobbin thread. Place star panels on top, so that charcoal thread is over burnt-orange edges and vice versa. Stitch over bottom edges of panels so that colours contrast. Leave a small hole in centre of roof.

5 Make a tassel by wrapping a length of each thread colour around 4 fingers, 5 times. Use a needle and thread to secure loop, bind threads together, secure with a stitch and run needle back to secured end (fig 3). Push secured end into centre of roof and catch in place with a few stitches. Trim ends of tassel.

roof triangle

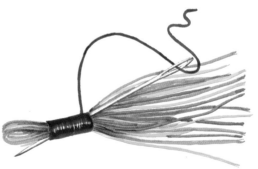

fig 3

embroidery without a foot

Free machine embroidery, worked without a foot, extends the techniques acquired for free stitching with a darning foot. The methods used overcome some of the difficulties encountered when using a darning foot. The main advantage to stitching without a foot is that it allows a clear view of the stitching area. Also, an embroidery hoop is almost invariably used, holding the fabric flat and restricting the hand position to holding the frame, so that there is little danger of stitching through a finger.

Most designs can be worked with or without a darning foot, so it really is a matter of personal preference, but do experiment with some free embroidery without a foot, as it may suddenly reveal all kinds of new possibilities in your work. A selection of designs on which to practise is given on pages 100–101.

Using a hoop

fig 1

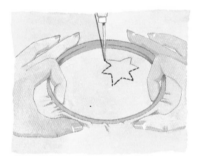

fig 2

It is essential to stretch the fabric tightly and evenly while machine embroidering, and the easiest way of doing this is to use an embroidery hoop. Wooden hoops are the most suitable as they grip the fabric very tightly, although other types can improved by binding (see page 16).

• Fix the fabric in the reverse manner to that used for hand embroidery, with the working surface (right side) at the bottom of the frame, so that the underside lies flat against the machine bed for stitching (see page16).
• Choose a comfortable position for holding the hoop. This depends to a degree on its size, but as the movement of the hoop controls the stitching it is important to find the position which ensures maximum control. Try one of the two methods shown in figs 1 and 2, and do not grip the hoop too tightly – an absorbing design may require long periods of stitching, and clenched fingers will create aches and tension in your hands, arms and shoulders.
• For some projects a hoop size has been given, but it is a guide rather than a command: use the size of hoop which is most comfortable to hold. For small areas it is advisable to have the complete design within the ring, but for larger pieces it is much easier to use a smaller hoop and move the fabric as necessary than to try to manœuvre a wheel!
• Before transferring a design on to fabric, ensure that there is a sufficient fabric allowance around the design to fix it into the hoop. Position the area to be worked in the centre of the hoop.

Setting up the machine

Set up the machine as for free stitching with a darning foot (see pages 44–45), but without a foot. Setting up the machine, lowering or covering the teeth and setting the stitch length and tension soon becomes automatic, but until it does always run through the sequence of changing the machine from set to free stitching. When using an unfamiliar machine or one which has been unused for a while, work a few lines of set straight stitch on waste fabric to ensure that the machine is running smoothly and correctly, and then change over to the free-stitching settings.

Starting to stitch

The technique for free embroidery is just the same as that used for free stitching with a darning foot: the stitch length is set to 0 and the teeth are lowered, so it is the movement of the hoop which will determine the stitch length and direction.

1 It is vital to lower the presser bar before starting to stitch, otherwise the top tension will not be engaged. The loose threads are more likely to tangle, so bring both to the top of the fabric and hold them behind the needle.

2 As you begin, secure the threads by either stitching on the spot a few times or by using reverse stitching.

3 Become accustomed to working at medium speed, as working slowly actually increases control problems. Concentrate on moving the hoop, first stitching straight lines in different directions and then building up confidence with curves and circles.

4 Secure the threads at the end. When changing the top colour only, leave the bobbin thread uncut but stitch on the spot as before to secure the new colour.

Technical stitching problems such as needle and thread breakages are more likely with free embroidery. If the machine is running well for set stitching it is probably your technique that is at fault, so refer to Problem solving, below.

Embroidery techniques

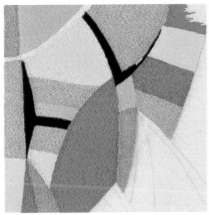

The techniques detailed here are equally suitable for working with or without a darning foot. Try both methods, following the general instructions for both to determine which feels most comfortable.

• Start with combinations of straight lines. Work parallel lines by moving the hoop up and down or from side to side. Make the lines closer and closer together, until they form a solid block.
• Move the hoop in small curves and circles, creating loops and wiggles. Vermicelli stitch (top left), which is worked as a series of semi-circles stitched in alternate directions, creates an interesting texture. Lots of tiny circles worked close together and overlapping each other create a filling stitch called seed stitch (centre left).
• Practise methods of outlining shapes. Work freehand or over a pencilled line, and compare the effect of one line of outline stitching with two or more.
• Work blocks of solid colour within the outlines. Practise creating a dense area of stitching with no fabric showing.
• Work several blocks of colour, at first stitching up to the outline and then over it, so that the areas of colour meet neatly with no outline showing.
• Blocks of stitching can be worked in different directions, creating interesting shading as the light reflects off the embroidery threads in different ways. However, stitching blocks at different angles tends to distort the fabric, so if the finished embroidery needs to be flat and cannot easily be stretched or mounted, it is safer to work all the blocks with parallel lines of stitching.

• Experiment with using different colours together, and with enhancing a palette of colour by introducing a complete contrast, such as black (bottom left).

Problem solving
• If the top thread breaks, it may be being held too tightly as stitching starts, or the top tension may need to be loosened slightly. Alternatively, the thread may be looping into the bobbin case and breaking. Check the underside for loops and then tighten the top tension if necessary.
• If the bobbin thread is not holding, check to see if it has broken. If not, the fabric may be too loose in the hoop. Natural fabrics are easier to stitch than synthetics, but using a ballpoint or thicker needle often solves the problem.
• Machine embroidery threads are not as tough as sewing threads, and may break when being forced into heavily worked areas or tough fabrics. Using a larger needle may help.
• Blunt needles will skip stitches, so change them before they bend or break. As a guide, the Book Binder on pages 56–59 would need at least three replacement needles.

If the needle breaks continually, either it is being pulled by attempting to make stitches that are too big, or the needle has been inserted in the machine back to front or not high enough.

silk lampshade

A machine-embroidered design need not be complicated or time-consuming to work. Sometimes a very simple application can be equally – or even more – effective than a heavily worked one. Here, softly layered drapes of silk and organza are caught together with small spots of vermicelli stitching. The choice of colours is all-important, so spend time laying different tones of organza over the underlayer of silk dupion. This shade is a combination of three spicy colours from the same palette, but contrasts – such as blue over red to create purple, or two similar fabric colours highlighted with contrasting spots of embroidery – could be just as effective. Before stitching, the organza is cut away at the points to be embroidered to reveal the true colour of the silk below.

Stitch method

Set straight stitch
Set zigzag stitch
Free straight stitch
Tension: normal settings throughout
Foot: normal presser foot for
    making up
Needles: 12/80

You will need

To cover a lampshade 25.5cm (10in)
in diameter and 15cm (6in) deep:
White or cream lampshade
80 x 100cm (32 x 39in) silk
    dupion
90cm (36in) square organza
1 reel toning rayon machine
    embroidery thread
Sewing threads to match silk and
    organza
Tape or ribbon
Small embroidery hoop
Fabric glue

To cut out

1 Fabrics to cover lampshade are cut as complete circles. Measure 2 sides and across top of lampshade (A, A and B in fig 1) and add together. Add another 15cm (6in) for extra fullness and hems: total is diameter of silk circle.

2 Place one end of a length of tape in centre of silk and pin. Measure half diameter length along tape from pin and mark. Hold central pin and rotate taut tape, drawing a circle on silk with a soft pencil held at marked point on tape (fig 2). In centre of circle, mark a circle 3cm (1¼in) less in diameter than measurement B on fig 1. Cut out around both circles.

3 Add 5cm (2in) to larger silk circle diameter, then halve this measurement and mark a circle on organza as above (if pencil will not work on organza, mark circle with pins). Mark a central circle to same size as for silk. Cut out around both circles.

fig 1

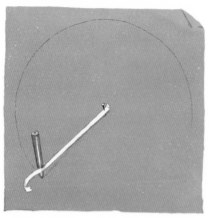

fig 2

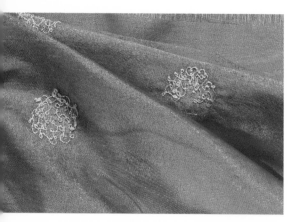

To work the embroidery

1 Fold silk circle in half, in half again and in half once more. Finger-press along folds, so that when circle is unfolded, 8 creases at even intervals are obvious.

2 Lay organza circle over silk with an even overlap all round, and pin together along creases with 3 evenly spaced pins on each. On alternate creases, first pin should be about 2cm (¾in) further away from circle centre (fig 3). These pins mark positions of embroidered dots, so lay fabric circles over shade to check that positions fall within desired shade area.

3 At each pinned position, cut a 12mm (½in) diameter hole *in organza only*.

4 Set sewing machine for free embroidery, with teeth covered or lowered, no foot, tension normal, and stitch length and zigzag set to 0. Thread top and bobbin with toning embroidery thread. Place fabrics in embroidery hoop with a hole in centre, and stitch over hole with vermicelli stitch (page 51). Stitching should extend beyond cut edge of hole and hold fabrics together. Stitch all the dots.

To make up

1 Set sewing machine for set stitching, with teeth up, normal presser foot, tension normal and stitch length set to 3. Change top and bobbin thread to sewing thread to match silk.

2 Measure circumference of silk circle, and cut out enough bias strips 3cm (1¼in) wide from remainder of silk to make a hem facing 8cm (3in) longer than circle circumference. With right sides together, join short ends of strips (fig 4), then press and trim seam allowances. With right sides together and cut edges even, lay bias strip around edge of silk circle. Pin, overlapping ends and folding short cut edge of underneath end to wrong side, then stitch around circle with a 1.5cm (⅝in) seam allowance.

3 Trim seam allowance. Fold over and press a narrow turning along unstitched edge of facing, then press facing to wrong side of silk. Hand sew folded edge to silk with invisible slip stitches.

4 Finish organza edge by setting zigzag to 3, using sewing thread to match

fig 3

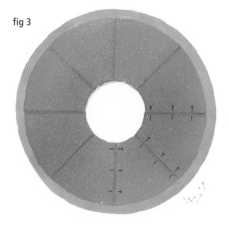

fig 4

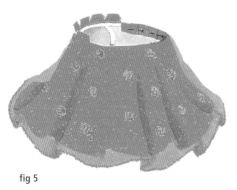

fig 5

organza and stitching just inside outer edge on right side – this will automatically roll organza. Trim away excess fabric.

5 Lay circles centrally over lampshade and make a series of cuts from central hole to just short of inside edge of shade (fig 5). Remove from shade, fold organza and silk together to wrong side of silk and pin. Lay over central hole to check that folded edge will fold neatly to inside of hole; it may be necessary to lengthen some cuts. Catch cut edges to inside with hand stitches.

6 Apply a circle of fabric glue sparingly around top inside edge of lampshade and, following manufacturer's instructions, lightly press inner circle of fabrics on to glue. Apply tiny spots of glue to lampshade to hold silk to it in even folds; glue spots should fall under lines of stitched dots.

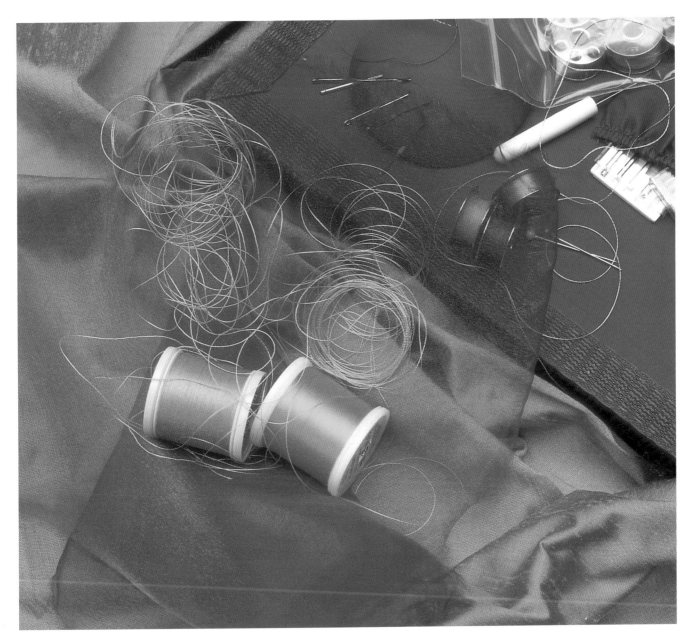

book binder

A large piece such as this cover for a ring binder or similar-sized book may appear daunting by virtue of its size, but once you have practised a free-stitching filling technique and feel confident creating a block of colour, it is simply a matter of 'colouring in'. Filling the various areas of colour and gradually building up the design will then become a rhythmic and absorbing process. Work all the coloured areas first and add the black blocks afterwards, to create a strong contrast which will give definition to the design.

The method of stitching described is totally free, without any foot, which allows a clear view of the stitching and build-up of colour, but if you find footless stitching frightening, use a darning foot. As the finished embroidery will not be stretched or mounted, it is important to choose a firm fabric and to stitch all the coloured blocks with the stitching lines following the grain of the fabric to prevent distortion.

Stitch methods
Set straight stitch
Free straight stitch
Tension: normal settings throughout
Foot: normal presser foot for making up
Needle: 14/90

You will need
To cover a 23 x 17.5cm (9 x 7in) ring binder:
80cm (1yd) medium-weight calico, 90cm (36in) wide
20 x 45cm (8 x 18in) thin wadding
Cotton sewing thread in 100m (109yd) reels:
    4 reels lime green
    3 reels each eau-de-nil, jasmine yellow, flame and gold
Cotton machine embroidery thread in 200m (217yd) reels:
    2 reels each black and bright yellow
Cream sewing thread
17cm (7in) embroidery hoop
Fabric glue

Placement plan.

To work the embroidery

1 Enlarge pattern outline, which shows cover front and half of spine, on page 59 to 110% using a photocopier. Check that outer line of design is at least 6mm (¼ in) larger than ring binder to allow for some contraction. For cover back, trace design once again. Reverse tracing and tape to left-hand side of spine (see placement plan on left).

2 Cut calico into 2 35 x 63cm (13¾ x 24¾in) rectangles. With marked grain line on straight grain of fabric, lay one rectangle centrally over pattern, with a wide margin of calico all round, and trace off design.

3 Place top right-hand corner of design in embroidery hoop. Set sewing machine for free stitching, with teeth lowered or covered, no foot, and stitch length and zigzag set to 0. Thread top and bobbin with matching thread, and work each coloured section by first outlining shape, then filling by stitching up and down parallel to shorter edges of calico. Remember always to lower foot lever before stitching, even though there is no foot (see page 50).

4 Fill in black sections after surrounding coloured shapes have been embroidered. Because black sections are mostly smaller and finer, fill with stitches in whichever direction is most appropriate.

5 Embroider any border areas within hoop with stitches parallel to edges of ring binder.

6 Move hoop along and repeat steps 3–5 until front of cover is complete. Then stitch back of cover, and finally spine.

7 Lay finished embroidery over design pattern. It will have contracted: bring back to its original size by increasing border widths.

8 Press embroidery, first on wrong and then on right side, using a steam iron on cotton setting.

To assemble the cover

1 Cut 2 rectangles of wadding to fit patterned sections (without borders) and use a minimal dab of fabric glue in centre of each patterned section to secure wadding in place.

2 With right sides together and edges even, lay embroidered rectangle on second calico rectangle. Trim long top and bottom edges to leave 1.5cm (⅝ in) seam allowances. On each short edge, measure 9.5 cm (3¾ in) beyond embroidery, mark and trim.

3 Set sewing machine for set stitching, with teeth up, normal presser foot, tension normal and stitch length set to 3. Using cream sewing thread, stitch together side seams 1.5cm (⅝ in) in from cut edges (fig 1). With calico pieces lying perfectly flat, measure exactly 8cm (3¼ in) in from each stitching line and make a mark.

4 Create a pleat at one end of embroidery as shown in fig 2.

5 With wrong side of embroidery up, stitch along one long side on very edge of embroidery. Repeat along second side, leaving an 18cm (7in) gap for turning (fig 3).

6 Turn through, press and oversew gap by hand.

fig 1

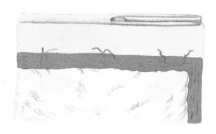

fig 2

fig 3

Enlarge to 110% on a
photocopier.

■ black   □ jasmine yellow   ■ bright yellow   ■ gold   ▨ flame   □ eau-de-nil   ■ lime green

free satin stitch

Using the stitch-width, or zigzag, control to alter the width of the stitch, while continuing to control the length manually (by moving the fabric or hoop), gives rise to a whole new range of embroidery techniques. While initial attempts to alter the width settings and control the size and direction of stitching may leave you longing for another pair of hands, do persevere – there is a wealth of exciting effects which can be created by using the satin-stitch setting range.

Starting to stitch

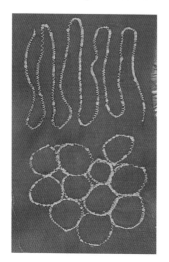

Always use an embroidery hoop for free zigzag and satin stitching, firstly because the fabric is far more likely to twist and pucker with the effect of the swing needle, and secondly because the fabric may have to be moved with one hand only, and making controlled movements single-handed without a hoop is virtually impossible.

1 Start (and end) each line of zigzag or satin stitch by working a few straight stitches in one spot.
2 To begin with, set the stitch width and practise controlling the stitch length – uneven stitching will be much more obvious when using swing-needle settings. You will need to be able to create an even zigzag effect before attempting satin stitch, which is formed by moving the hoop so slowly that the stitches lie side by side.
3 Work a series of exaggerated loops, and then circles. Note that although the hoop can be moved in any direction, the swing needle only works from side to side, so the effect of the zigzag stitching is much more obvious when the hoop is being moved forwards and backwards than when it is being moved sideways.
4 Begin to alter the width settings, first working blocks of different widths and then altering the dial with your right hand as the hoop is being moved with your left, to create a graduated widening and narrowing.

For maximum control of the hoop, hold it with your left hand at the back (behind the needle) and your left arm resting on the machine bed.

Embroidery techniques

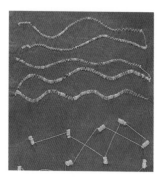

The Button Collection on pages 62–63 simply uses a zigzag setting to increase the dimpled effect of the filling stitch, but swing-needle settings can be used to create a great variety of effects, from an abstract pattern covering the fabric to small overstitched areas adding texture to straight-stitched embroidery. A range of outlines on which to practise is given on pages 102–103.

• Practise straight lines, both forwards and backwards, then experiment with creating wavy lines, working rows of lines side by side.
• Try working rows of satin stitch and then overstitching between them with a narrow width setting.
• Work satin-stitch beads by securing threads with straight stitching on the spot, then setting the desired width and again stitching on the spot until a raised bead is created. Secure the thread, move to the next bead point and repeat.
• Any automatic pattern settings on a machine can be stitched in a free way.

Problem solving
• The most likely problem with free satin stitch is that the top thread may pull the bobbin thread to the surface (see opposite). If the effect is not desirable, loosen the top tension slightly. If the looser stitching style suits the embroidery, highlight it by using a contrasting bobbin thread.
• Turning neat corners while stitching may prove difficult. If so, stop stitching when the needle is inserted through the fabric on the outside point of the corner, and pivot the hoop around the needle before starting to stitch again.

tension techniques

With set stitching it is usually desirable to have an even top and bobbin tension and, as anyone who has ever attended needlework classes knows, to alter the tension settings on a sewing machine is to court disaster! Contrary to belief, however, altering the tension settings will not adversely affect the smooth running of the machine afterwards – they can simply be reset. For machine embroiderers, using unusual tension techniques is a fascinating way of adding shades of colour and texture to their work.

Simple tension changes

For guidance on achieving perfect tension and on how to alter both top and bobbin tension, see page 11. There are some embroidery techniques for which it is desirable to have a tight bobbin tension that will pull the top threads to the underside of the work and these are described in detail on pages 92–93. But for the more gentle textural effects created in this chapter the bobbin thread is drawn up to appear on the top of the work, and this can usually be achieved by tightening the top tension only.

Starting to stitch

Always start by stitching a test row with normal tensions to use as a control, and remember to look at the underside of the stitching as well as the top surface to see what effects the altered tension settings are creating.

1 Mount the fabric in an embroidery hoop – this is essential.
2 For practice stitching, thread the top and bobbin with the same thread but in contrasting colours. This will make it much easier to judge the effects as each tension is altered.
3 If only a small alteration is required, it is quicker and easier to alter the top tension only, but tightening one tension and not compensating by loosening the other may cause the unaltered thread to snap more often, especially as the tension is increased. If the thread begins to snap, loosen the bobbin tension to compensate for the tightened top tension.
4 Hold the threads towards the back of the machine when starting to stitch, otherwise the bobbin thread will not be under tension and may well loop up on the back of the work.
5 When you have finished embroidering, readjust the tension settings to normal.

Embroidery techniques

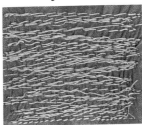

The tension techniques described here are intended to be subtle. They are used to create shades of colour and a dimpled texture on the Button Collection on pages 62–65, and could be used to create a similar textural effect in the grassy area of Lying on a Rug on pages 66–69.

• The filling stitch on the buttons has a tightened top tension which, when used with contrasting threads at top and bobbin, creates a speckled texture. Choosing a zigzag setting of 1 or 2 will create a more random stitching effect.
• Use a fast stitch speed and move the hoop slowly to create a filling stitch suitable for the buttons or picture.
• Reversing the top and bobbin colours creates a subtle change. Using matching threads gives a more intense colour.

Problem solving

• Stitching on the spot can create decorative bobbles but will increase the likelihood of the thread snapping.
• If the bobbin tension is too tight it will pull the top thread down into loops, which may catch in the shuttle race.
• For free satin stitch with a tightened top tension, loosening the bobbin tension creates a softer effect, whereas tightening the top tension only can create a rather mean, taut top line.

61

button collection

Like the box panels on pages 46–49, button covers are an ideal project on which to practise new techniques or experiment with different designs. They can be worked on small scraps from your workbasket, or on a lightweight calico or similar fabric. Choose a limited range of colours – seven or eight is ideal – and work each button using a selection of three colours from the palette, plus a metallic thread to add a rich, jewel-like quality.

Use the individual designs to experiment with the top tension; use one colour in the top and another in the bobbin; try different tensions; then reverse the top and bottom colours – all this will build up your knowledge of the multitude of shades and textures which can be created using a limited range of colours. The completed buttons will form a complementary set of individual designs, and can be used to enliven a dull cushion or dress up a plain jacket. Alternative designs can be found on pages 108–109.

Stitch methods
Free straight stitch
Free satin stitch
Tension: normal or top only
    tightened
Foot: darning foot
Needle: 12/80 or 10/70

You will need
Light calico or similar fabric scraps
Sheer fabric scraps (organza is ideal)
Assorted machine embroidery threads
Gold metallic machine embroidery
    thread
Embroidery hoop
Easy-cover buttons
Card for templates

To prepare the fabric
1 For each size of easy-cover button, 3 circular card templates are needed: 1 with diameter equal to that of button (area of main design); 1 with diameter 6mm (¼in) larger (allows design to continue and cover sides); 1 with diameter 12mm (½in) larger (extra to be clipped into back of button to hold fabric in place). Using a compass and pencil, draw and cut out 3 appropriate cardboard circles.
2 For each button, use templates to draw 3 concentric circles on calico. Draw one of the designs above left into central circle, choose an alternative from pages 108–109, or make your own design.

3 Set sewing machine for free stitching with a darning foot, with teeth lowered or covered. Set stitch length and zigzag to 0, and thread top and bobbin with embroidery thread to match the chosen colour of organza.
4 Fix calico in hoop. Cut organza piece slightly larger than largest circle and lay it over it. Stitch around the 2 larger circles to hold organza in place.

To work the embroidery
1 Change either top or bobbin thread to a contrasting colour, then tighten top tension, set zigzag to 1 or 2 if desired, and fill in all areas of one colour. Change one of the thread colours and fill in next area of colour.
2 Continue changing colours and filling in until design is complete. On some buttons, areas of organza can be left unstitched or a motif can be added over base stitching.
3 Thread top and bobbin with gold thread, loosen top tension again and, with zigzag set to 0, separate areas of colour with lines of straight stitch. Motifs can be highlighted with 2 or more lines of straight stitching.

To make up
Cut out around outer calico circle and, following manufacturer's instructions, catch fabric on to serrated under-edge of button front and clip on back (fig 1).

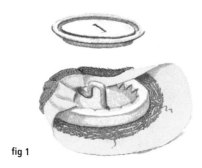

fig 1

picture techniques

Embroidering a picture is only frightening because it changes the project from a practical one requiring certain machining skills into an artistic achievement. If you find the idea of stitching a picture more challenging than stitching a pattern, think of the picture simply as outlines to fill in, and adding the fine details merely as features or decorations on top. The style of the finished picture is entirely personal, but to begin with, simple naïve drawings are the easiest to translate into an embroidered work, as they use blocks of colour and strong outlines.

Stitching a picture

The stitching used for a picture can include some or all of the techniques described earlier in this chapter. The fabric should be held in an embroidery hoop and the machine set up for free stitching, with or without a darning foot.

Whether to use only straight stitch and a normal tension setting, or to introduce some satin stitching and tightened top tension, is a personal choice. It is tempting to use the same bobbin thread throughout, but changing it to match the top thread will create more intense colours.

1 For a small picture, centre the design in the hoop; for a larger picture, which will need to be moved within the hoop as areas are completed, begin stitching near the centre and move outwards to avoid distorting the fabric too much.

2 Work the outlines first, using black or dark grey thread. There is no need to cut the threads between outlines as they are stitched. When the outlines have been completed, trim away loose threads on the right side and leave on the reverse.

3 Work each block of colour just up to its dark outline – if some outlines are visible on the final picture they will simply look like sketch lines. Practise joining blocks of colour neatly: it is a mistake to stitch around each outlined area with the self colour, as this will create separate blocks. These could be effective on the Book Binder (see pages 56–59), but would detract from a picture.

4 Within each area of colour, concentrate on working parallel lines of stitches to create a neat colouring technique, but alter the direction of stitching of different areas to suit the design. For instance, where the girl's legs bend (above left), curve the lines of stitching to follow the contours.

Techniques for larger areas

You can work the areas of background around objects in the picture as they are completed, which will leave you with less monotonous stitching to do at the end but does not allow for any late changes to the design. Alternatively, you can leave all the background until the rest of the picture is complete, and then decide whether the plain background needs to be a slightly different colour to that originally planned, or if the use of a tightened top tension would add some desirable texture.

By tightening the top tension (see page 61) and using the same colour at top and bobbin, a slight texture can be added to a single-coloured area. Using a contrasting bobbin colour with the tension technique could create a range of other effects – for example, try a silver bobbin thread with dark blue for a starry sky, or green with a yellow bobbin thread for a field of buttercups.

If filling in large areas of colour is daunting, cheat! You can work the embroidery on a suitable coloured fabric, appliqué pieces of coloured fabric in place, or use fabric paints to colour the background areas.

Working fine details

There are two methods of working details such as facial features. You can either work them first and fill in the stitching around them, or wait until all the other stitching is done and then work the details.

If the details are worked first, there is a much better chance of unpicking them successfully if they do go wrong – unpicking small stitches which are worked into a mass of other stitches is practically impossible to achieve. However, there is a danger that the finer details will disappear under the surrounding stitches. Details that are worked on top of the background stitches will be raised slightly and therefore look more prominent.

Whichever method is used, it is safest to pull both the threads at the start and finish off each piece of stitching to the reverse, tying the threads together to ensure that they are secured.

Finishing edges

There are two methods of finishing picture edges. The first method can be used for pictures with straight edges, while the second is more suitable for pictures with uneven edges, which machine embroidered pieces often have.

g 1

g 2

• For the first method, iron double-sided hemming tape along the four edges of the embroidery on the reverse side of the picture, trim the fabric to the width of the hemming tape and fold it over so that the picture edge is just rolled to the back. Carefully trim away excess fabric at the corners and press to adhere (fig 1).
• For the second finishing method, tack some strips of tear-away fabric stabilizer or vanishing muslin (see page 80) over the four edges on the reverse side of the picture (fig 2). Turn the picture over so it is right side up.

Then, for both methods, set the sewing machine for set satin stitch, with teeth up, normal presser foot and tension, stitch length set at 1 and zigzag at 4. Stitch carefully all round the outer edge of the picture. If the outer edges are folded under, the outside stitch of the satin stitch should be worked over the folded edge. If the edges are unfolded (the second method above), the inside stitch of the satin stitch should be worked over the edge of the picture stitching all the way round. Tear away the stabilizer or vanishing muslin and trim the fabric to the satin stitch.

Problem solving

• Rest the machine every 20 minutes to ensure that it does not overheat.
• Change the needles before they bend, break or become blunt – blunt needles will skip stitches.
• If the work has become distorted during the stitching process, press it under a barely damp cloth. Do not press heavily, as the weight will flatten the embroidered stitches.
• If the work is very distorted, dampen and stretch it (see page 19) and leave to dry completely before lacing it over mounting card.

lying on a rug

Embroidering a figurative picture might seem an impossible achievement, but the embroidery techniques are actually no different to those used for the Book Binder or Button Collection projects earlier in this chapter. The secret of success is to start small and to practise. Enlarge and trace the cat, two or three potted plants or the head from the design on page 69, draw a square or rectangle around the outline and stitch on to calico stretched in an embroidery hoop. The practice pieces can be mounted and used as greetings cards. Skills at filling areas of colour and working fine details will be quickly acquired – continue to work small, simple pictures, drawing inspiration from postcards, pictures or photographs, and you will gradually build up the skills and confidence to embroider a large picture.

Stitch methods

Free straight stitch
Set straight stitch
Tension: normal or top only tightened
Foot: darning foot, normal presser
    foot
Needle: 12/80

You will need

For a finished picture 20 x 26cm
(8 x 10¼in):
40 x 50cm (16 x 20in) heavyweight
    calico
1 reel each rayon machine embroidery
    thread in colours shown on chart,
    plus 1 extra reel background green
1 reel multicolour rayon machine
    embroidery thread, for stripes on
    ginger cat
1 reel silver metallic machine embroidery
    thread, for cat's whiskers
5 skeins stranded cottons in colours to
    co-ordinate with picture
Black sewing thread
38.5 x 45cm (15¼ x 18in) mounting card
20cm (8in) wooden embroidery hoop
Iron-on hemming web or tear-away
    fabric stabilizer

To work the embroidery

1 Enlarge picture outlines on the right to 110% using a photocopier and then transfer centrally on to calico using a sharp pencil. Stretch calico into embroidery hoop.

2 Set sewing machine for free stitching with a darning foot, teeth lowered or covered, tension normal and black thread at top and bobbin. Work all the outlines first.

3 Following key and diagram opposite, fill in blocks of colour, always using same colour thread at top and bobbin. Alter top tension if desired for some areas (see page 61).

4 Move hoop and continue to fill areas of colour until picture is complete.

5 Finish picture edges using one of the methods described on page 65.

6 Hold long lengths of stranded cottons together. Starting a small way in from one corner of picture, hold lengths against picture edge and lightly twist them together to form a cord. Set sewing machine for set stitching, with stitch length and zigzag set at 4, and zigzag over cord, attaching it to picture with outside stitch of zigzag (fig 1). Fold cord crisply around corners. Overlap cord ends neatly, so that cut edges all lie under picture on reverse side (fig 2).

To mount the picture

1 Lay picture centrally on mounting card. With pencil point under twisted cord (so line will be hidden), draw around edge of picture.

2 With a sewing needle, pierce holes at 1.5m (½ in) intervals and, using black sewing thread, lace picture to card with tiny stitches into reverse edge of picture and long stitches under mounting card.

fig 1

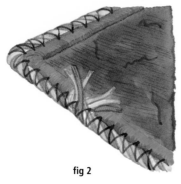

fig 2

Enlarge to 110% on a photocopier.

- ■ black *cat, girl's and ginger cat's features*
- ■ bright pink *girl's cheeks, rug border and trowel handle*
- □ pale pink *skin tone*
- ■ dark brown *hair*

- ■ mid brown *earth*
- ■ terracotta *flowerpots*
- □ blue-grey *trowel*
- ■ pale grey *black cat's features*
- □ ochre *ginger cat, spots on earth*

- ■ violet *dress*
- ■ blue *stripes on rug*
- ■ emerald *spots on rug*
- ■ mid green *grass*
- ■ jade *plants*

- ■ dark green *lines on grass and edging*
- ■ gold *rug*
- ■ multicolour *stripes on ginger cat*
- □ silver *whiskers*

69

Decorative effects

Learning to free stitch opens up a wonderful variety of effects with which lines can be worked or blocks of colour created. This final chapter explores the additional possibilities for unusual stitch effects which are offered by altering the stitch tension settings, or by stitching on vanishing fabric.

In perfect set stitching, the top and bobbin threads twist within the fabric so that no top thread appears below and no bobbin thread on top. Altering the tension settings allows one thread to pull the other through the fabric, forming raised lines or exaggerated loops far removed from the sedate progression of set stitches.

Vanishing fabrics, as the name implies, provide a temporary surface on which to stitch. This is then removed, leaving the stitches to form a new fabric. All kinds of designs can be worked using this technique, from precise grids to insubstantial lacy wisps, or rich embroidered tapestries which it is hard to believe could be stitched by an ordinary sewing machine!

letters &
monograms

Mention machine embroidery, and monograms on towels or bathrobes immediately spring to mind. In fact, the very wide, graduated lines of a traditional satin-stitch monogram can only be created with an industrial machine or a computerized domestic model. However, although it is impossible to reproduce those flat satin-stitch letters, there are a variety of other ways of stitching decorative lettering using any swing-needle sewing machine, and the handwritten quality of the letters creates a particularly charming effect.

Choosing letters

On pages 104–105 there is a choice of alphabets, including one of capitals which could be used for initials, and a flowing, lower-case script which would be ideal for embroidering a message on a drawstring bag, adding simple detail in self-coloured thread on bed- or tablelinen, or working an apt quote on a cushion or chairback. Alternatively, use either your own handwriting or that of the person to whom you will be giving the finished piece and enlarge it on a photocopier to an appropriate size. As a guide, the small letters on the Pieced Tablecloth on pages 74–79 are 2cm (¾in) high.

Stitching techniques

The lettering styles shown on these two pages are much more free flowing and personal than an industrially stitched monogram, but it is still important that each letter should be distinct – a single line of straight stitch, for example, would fade into insignificance on all but the smallest project. The first method given here is couching, which uses set machine stitching, while all the other methods employ free stitching.

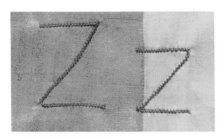

Set-stitched couching.

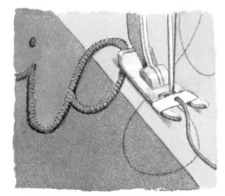

fig 1

Set-stitched letters with couching
Set-stitched letters tend to be very angular. One of the simplest ways of creating a more flowing script is to sew a length of fine cord over the lines of the letters, using set stitching with a zigzag width slightly wider than the cord. Sew over but not through the cord, so that it is caught, or 'couched', in place.
• Some machines have a cording foot, which holds the cord in the correct position while stitching; if your machine does not have this facility, wrap sticky tape around an open-toe presser foot, set the correct zigzag width to couch the cord and pierce a hole in the tape so that the cord lies in the centre of the stitching (fig 1). Use a very thin cord, such as pearl

cotton or a silk yarn, and feed it from above, through the hole in the tape or the cording foot and out under the foot to the back: the cord will then be couched down in the right place automatically.
• The length of the stitch can be altered to create different effects, or you can use contrasting threads or even a monofilament nylon thread, which would be almost invisible.
• With fine fabrics, it may be necessary to use a tear-away stabilizer under the stitching to prevent puckering.
   When stitching is complete, thread the ends of the cord into a large-eyed needle and pull through to the wrong side of the fabric.

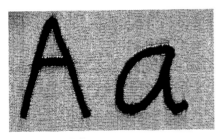

Corded satin stitch

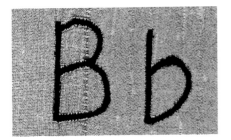

Satin stitch

Straight stitch

Compound whip stitch

Free-stitched letters

The lettering techniques below can be adapted to create any size of lettering. For all of them, the machine should be set up for free stitching, with the teeth lowered or covered, the stitch length at 0 and no foot. The first two are worked with satin stitch and the rest with straight stitch.

Fix the fabric in an embroidery hoop for ease of manœuvring and use a fairly thick needle: 14/90 or 16/100. Always fix the starting and finishing stitches with a few stitches on the spot.

Corded satin stitch This technique uses a very fine cord, such as pearl embroidery cotton or string.

1 Lay the cord over the lettering and first of all couch it in place by hand to secure it.

2 Set the zigzag width to between 3 and 5 (it must be wider than the cord), then loosen the top tension and tighten the bobbin tension.

3 Stitch over the cord with evenly spaced satin stitch, so that the cord is completely covered.

The altered stitch tension should create a domed effect over the cord, forming a raised letter.

Satin stitch For a slightly finer letter, use uncorded satin stitch.

1 Again, loosen the top tension and tighten the bobbin tension.

2 Move the embroidery hoop slowly, so that the satin stitch forms evenly to create a strong line.

To form letters of an even width, the hoop may have to be turned through a full 360°. Moving the hoop sideways to work the horizontal parts of the letters will result in much finer lines, creating an italic lettering style.

Straight stitch This is the simplest stitch to use, as altering the direction of stitching will not affect the final width of the letter.

1 Again, loosen the top tension and tighten up the bobbin tension.

2 Work a few lines of straight stitch together. One line of stitching would be very fine; four or five lines are suitable for a letter 2cm (¾in) high.

Whip stitch This stitch will create a less solid letter than either of the satin-stitch methods, but because the stitching is raised it will be more defined than straight stitch.

1 This time, loosen the bobbin tension and tighten the top tension, so that the top thread lies on the fabric surface and the bobbin thread is pulled up through the fabric, to create a series of little loops on the surface. (For more information on whip stitch and tension effects in general, see pages 92–93.)

2 For a fine letter, work whip stitch as above, using only two rows together to form double whip stitch.

3 For a thicker letter, work a few lines of whip stitch together to create compound whip stitch.

Problem solving

• Working machine-stitched letters takes practice. In general, work a letter as you would write it. Be prepared to stop and work a second line separately – the line crossing an A, for example.

• Monograms, which consist of two or three letters together, are more attractive if the letters can be entwined in some way.

• Working lettering on a large piece of fabric, such as the tablecloth on the following pages, may involve manœuvring a large quantity of fabric at different angles. Try to roll up extra fabric and safety pin it together to reduce the bulk.

If it proves too difficult to manœuvre a large quantity of fabric, use the satin-stitch technique described above and create italic-style letters.

pieced tablecloth

Piece together subtly contrasting shades of silk and embroider them with an eclectic selection of motifs to create a cloth fit for a feast. Choose dishes from around the world, recreate a memorable meal, concentrate on a favourite food – be it fish, as on this cloth, or an indulgent spread of delicious patisserie – or gather together the tools of the trade (see pages 106–107) and recreate them with a mixture of straight and whip stitch. Finally, label each dish or implement with a flowing script.

Stitch methods

Set straight stitch
Free straight stitch
Free satin stitch
Whip stitch
Vermicelli stitch
Tension: normal and altered
Feet: normal presser foot for making up
Needles: 12/80, 16/100

You will need

For a tablecloth 122cm (48in) square:
4 30cm (12in) lengths silk dupion, 122cm (48in) wide, in yellow, orange, copper and peach
100cm (39in) gold silk dupion, 122cm (48in) wide
1 reel sewing thread, to piece silk together
Rayon machine embroidery threads in black, white, gold, silver, lemon, apricot, peach, beige, milk-chocolate and dark brown, light and dark grey, bottle green, olive green and ginger
23cm (9in) embroidery hoop
12cm (5in) square card template

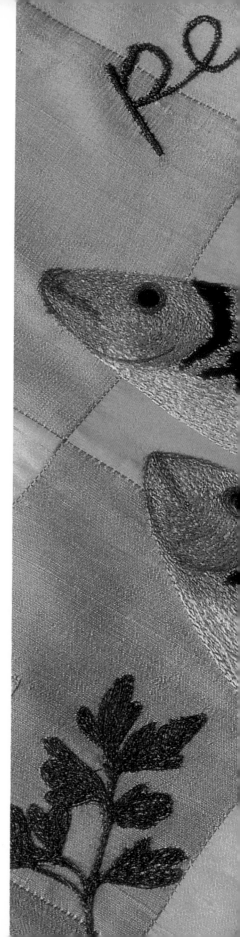

To make up the cloth

1 Machine wash all silk dupions on a wool setting. Press while still damp using a very hot, dry iron.

2 Cut out strips 12cm (5in) wide across fabric. Cut out 2 each from first 4 colours and 8 from gold. Use card template to mark strips into squares and cut out.

3 Form 12 strips of 12 squares, with a gold piece between each other colour. Using set straight stitch and smaller needle, stitch squares together with a 1cm (⅜in) seam allowance. Neaten seams and press open.

4 Lay strips together to form a large square and again stitch. Neaten and press seams open. Turn outer edges under twice to form a neat hem and stitch all round.

To work the embroidery

1 Set machine for free embroidery and insert larger needle. Enlarge food outlines on pages 78–79 to 156% and then to 110% using a photocopier. Transfer on to pieced fabric using a vanishing pen and following placement plan (below). Vanishing pens fade within 48 hours, so unless you are going to work very quickly, mark position of each dish lightly in pencil and then draw fine detail with a vanishing pen just before starting to embroider a dish.

2 Using alphabets on pages 104–105 or your own handwriting, draw lettering for each dish above it, again using pencil to mark its position and vanishing pen to add any detail.

3 Lettering is worked in satin stitch and food in a mixture of straight stitch, vermicelli stitch (see page 51) and whip stitch (see page 73). Use same colour thread at top and bobbin, unless a different bobbin thread would accentuate stitching. Large areas of colour are worked in straight stitch with a normal top and bobbin tension, with details added on top using either straight or vermicelli stitch in a contrasting colour, or whip stitch for a raised texture.

4 Ensure that all ends of threads are fixed with a few stitches on the spot. When embroidery is complete, cut off all loose ends and press firmly using a very hot steam iron.

Placement plan.

■ dark grey

░ light grey

▨ gold

■ bottle green

▨ olive green

▨ peach

▨ apricot

▨ ginger

▢ lemon

□ beige

▨ milk-chocolate brown

■ dark brown

■ black

□ white

▨ silver

canestrelli di chioggia
straight stitch, with whip stitch for outer shell
and gold filling

bouillabaisse de pêcheur
straight stitch, with vermicelli stitch for soup and
whip stitch on tentacles

spaghetti dela pina
straight stitch, with whip stitch for spaghetti,
shell details and leaves

pesce alla griglia
straight stitch, with minimal whip stitch on eyes,
cut lemon and leaves

antipasto acciughe alle olive
straight stitch for olives, with whip stitch for
detail on anchovies

moules à la marinière
straight stitch, with whip stitch on outer shells
and brown shading on *moules* detail

prawn satay
straight stitch, with whip stitch for prawn detail,
cut lemon and leaves, and satin stitch for skewers

assiette de fruits de mer
straight stitch, with whip stitch for prawn detail,
oyster shell and cut lemon

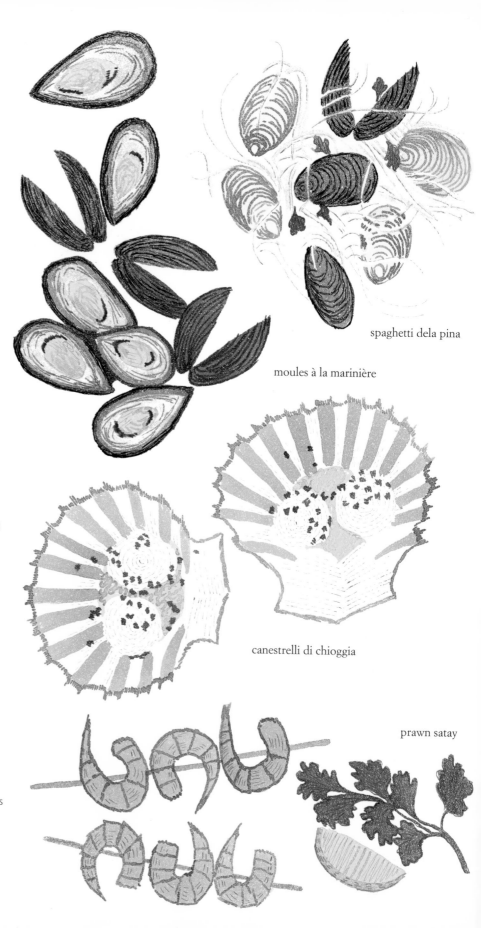

spaghetti dela pina

moules à la marinière

canestrelli di chioggia

prawn satay

pesce alla griglia

assiette de fruits de mer

antipasto acciughe alle olive

bouillabaisse

Enlarge to 156% and then to 110% on a photocopier.

79

vanishing fabrics

Machine embroidery is all about embellishing and adornment, adding decoration or creating wonderful effects, and the use of vanishing fabric takes the application of embroidery techniques one step further. Instead of embroidering on to a background fabric, the embroidery is worked on to one of three types of vanishing fabric, and once stitching is completed the fabric is 'vanished', leaving the stitches to form a new fabric which can be as airy or as dense as the embroiderer desires.

Choosing vanishing fabric

There are three types of vanishing fabric: vanishing muslin, and hot- and cold-water soluble fabrics. Each is quite distinctive in its properties, and all have definite advantages and disadvantages, but it is worth trying all three and deciding which one best suits your style of stitching.

All three fabrics are peculiar to machine embroidery and are not widely available. Try a well-stocked haberdashery department or craft supplier, or look for mail-order stockists in the advertisement section of specialist embroidery magazines.

Vanishing muslin

Vanishing muslin

Stiffened vanishing muslin was the first vanishing fabric to be developed. It can be used with or without an embroidery hoop and is a good choice for working a densely embroidered effect.

• Vanishing muslin is brittle, so if you wish to use it in a hoop fix it correctly at the first attempt, as trying to correct it may cause tearing.

• For stitching without a hoop, use a darning foot.

• Tension settings should be normal and the fabric moved at a medium pace.

• To create a solid stitched fabric use a darning technique, with lines of stitching worked across each other.

To vanish the muslin:

1 Place the design right side down on an old towel and press under a stationary dry iron, set on the highest heat setting. The muslin will first turn brown and then black.

2 Remove the iron and allow the work to cool before handling. Rub the embroidery between your hands over a wastebasket until all traces of muslin have flaked away, or brush gently with a clean, old toothbrush. Pick out any resisting bits of muslin with tweezers.

The most common mistake when vanishing the muslin is not to apply enough heat. The muslin will vanish before any natural-fibre threads and most synthetic machine-embroidery threads would be damaged. Metallic threads would be affected if next to the heat source, but if they are used on the top of the work and it is pressed on the reverse, they should be fine.

Alternatively, heat an oven to 180°C (350°F), lay the work on a baking tray and bake for five to six minutes.

NB The dust from burnt vanishing muslin can be very irritating to asthma sufferers and may cause attacks. Also, vanishing muslin gives off an unpleasant chemical smell when heated, so work in a ventilated room.

Cold-water soluble fabric

Cold-water soluble fabric is made from seaweed. It resembles a sheet of plastic and can be rather fragile. Much cheaper than hot-water soluble fabric and more widely available, it is a good choice to create open lacy effects. Cold-water soluble fabric must be used in a hoop for free embroidery, as the movement of the teeth in set stitching would cause it to tear.

• Set stitch length at 0 and make even, medium-length stitches.

• Start by using fine machine-embroidery threads, as thicker threads may cause tearing. If a small area tears, simply pin a patch over it and proceed. If the fabric tears badly, lay the work over a double layer of the soluble fabric before continuing with the stitching.

Cold-water soluble fabric

• Straight stitch is the easiest to work, but zigzag and satin stitch are also possible. Cold-water soluble fabric is not really suitable for solid stitching, but to create small blocks work a supporting network of lines and stitch over them.

To dissolve the fabric:

1 Place the work in a bowl of cold water and agitate it gently, or hold it under a running tap. If the threads will allow, lukewarm water will dissolve the fabric more quickly.

2 Agitating in a bowl will leave a residue of soluble fabric, which can be used as a stiffener to shape the fabric. If stiffened fabric is not required, rinse thoroughly and leave to dry on an old towel.

Hot-water soluble fabric

Hot-water soluble fabric looks like a very fine silk fabric. By far the most versatile of the three vanishing fabrics for stitching purposes, it can be stretched in a hoop or used by itself for set stitching.

• Hot-water soluble fabric will take much heavier satin stitch or solid stitching than cold-water soluble fabric, but is much more expensive.

• It is strong enough to use as a base for appliqué and, as it will withstand a low ironing heat, other fabrics can be bonded on to it using bonding web. However, the dissolving process limits the choice of appliqué fabrics and threads to those which are colourfast and can withstand boiling or simmering. In fact, most machine-embroidery threads, except metallic, will withstand immersion in boiling water.

To dissolve the fabric:

1 Place the fabric in a bowl, pour a kettle of boiling water over it and agitate, then drain off the water and repeat the process about five times.

Alternatively, for stubborn fabric which has no delicate stitching or appliqué, place the fabric in a saucepan of simmering water and simmer gently for two minutes, then drain and repeat three times.

Another option is to lay the fabric in a large, shallow dish, cover with water and, using a low microwave setting, barely simmer the water. Remove the work as soon as the fabric starts to soften, and repeat with more water as necessary.

2 The work will look very crumpled and shrivelled when wet. It can either be dried flat and restored to shape by pressing or, if necessary, the piece can be stretched while still wet (see page 19).

Hot-water soluble fabric

Using vanishing fabrics

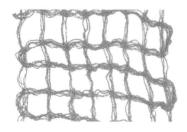

The main point to remember when stitching on any of the vanishing fabrics is that the stitching lines must cross to form an interconnecting net. If they do not, when the fabric is vanished the new fabric will simply unravel into one long line of stitches. So, whatever the final design, make sure that it is supported on a grid (see left) and that the interconnecting stitch is actually across another stitch, not alongside it.

• Lines of zigzag or satin stitch must be fixed by either working them over a line of straight stitch or stitching two or more lines of straight stitch on top of them.

• Try loosening the bobbin tension slightly so that the thread appears on the upper surface; exaggerated tension settings tend to look untidy.

• Work with different-coloured threads at top and bobbin. When the fabric is vanished, both will be visible.

• When working with an embroidery hoop, you will need to fit the whole design inside the hoop as the fabrics are likely to tear if repositioned.

Problem solving

• If the vanishing fabric is tearing or the stitches are unsatisfactory, try using a ballpoint needle or loosening top tension.

• Before cutting work out of a hoop and dissolving, hold it up to the light to check that the stitches are linked. If not, stitch a few more or the fabric will fall apart.

pins with panache

Work small blocks of colour in jewel-bright colours, surround or divide them with grids of gold or black, and create a closely worked fabric with all the richness of a medieval tapestry. Look at stained-glass windows, Persian carpets or Islamic mosaic work for intricate designs created with blocks of colour. Embellish the embroideries with a selection of beads and transform them into exotic pins to flaunt in a hat or display as a corsage. Alternative designs can be found on page 109.

Stitch methods

Free straight stitch
Free satin stitch
Hand beading
Tension: normal settings throughout
Feet: darning or embroidery foot
Needle: 12/80 or 14/90

You will need

20 x 20cm (8 x 8in) vanishing muslin
5 reels machine embroidery thread, in range of colours
1 reel gold metallic machine embroidery thread
1 reel sewing thread, in outline colour
Assorted beads to decorate
Hatpin and stopper or brooch back
Beading or fine hand-sewing needle
Super-glue gel (optional)

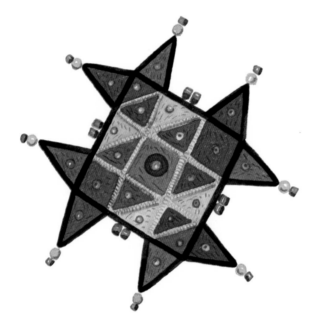

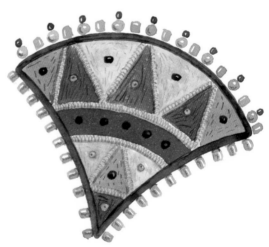

Design outlines are shown actual size.

To work the embroidery

1 Draw one of design outlines on page 82 on to vanishing muslin using a felt-tipped pen.

2 Set machine for free stitching, lower or cover teeth, and set stitch length and zigzag to 0. Choose an embroidery thread for outline, such as charcoal used here, and use that colour in bobbin throughout. Thread top with first colour of embroidery thread.

3 Start at centre of each block of colour and fill outline with stitches, using a darning technique. Work all blocks of one colour in design, straight stitching between blocks (fig 1).

4 Change top thread to second colour and work all areas of that colour. Repeat with further colours until all areas have been filled.

5 Change top thread to gold metallic, set zigzag to 2 and overstitch between blocks of colour to divide areas (fig 2).

6 Change top thread to outline colour, set zigzag width to 3 and overstitch around design outline (fig 3), finishing off securely at each end.

7 Burn away vanishing muslin using a hot iron (see page 80).

8 Thread beading or fine hand-sewing needle with a double thickness of sewing thread, make double stitches in centre on back of embroidery to secure thread, and then stitch on beads where shown on design outline. When beading is complete, secure end of thread with more double stitches and snip off remaining thread.

To make up

Slide decorative beads on to hatpin, lay pin across back of embroidery, and stitch in place with a double thickness of sewing thread. If embroidery is to be used as a brooch, stick brooch back in place with super-glue gel.

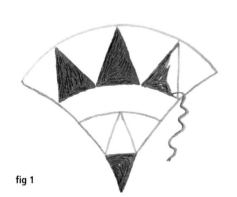

fig 1

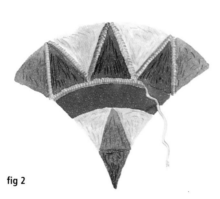

fig 2

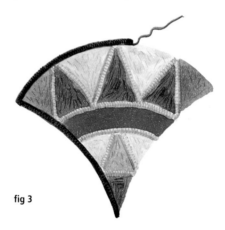

fig 3

dancing doll

Enter into the spirit of an Edwardian theatre with vanishing fabrics and glittering threads. Stitch a tiny rag doll and dress her in the finest gossamer costume, a shimmering web of embroidery topped with a bright, sparkling crown. Make her into a prima ballerina, or a slightly flushed chorus girl straight from the music halls. Allow your imagination full rein when embroidering her clothes, add wings for a magical Christmas fairy, minute stitched blossoms for a leading lady to hold, or lengthen her skirts into a sweeping train to transform her into a pouting princess.

Stitch method

Set straight stitch
Free straight stitch
Free satin stitch
Hand embroidery
Tension: normal settings throughout
Feet: normal presser foot
Needle: 11/80, 9/65

You will need

For a doll 18cm (7in) tall:
12 x 24cm (5 x 9½in) fine cotton fabric for body (a piece of old shirt dyed pale pink is ideal)
14cm (5½in) square pink satin for legs
Pink silk and stiffening-fabric scraps
10cm (4in) ivory fine veiling net, 90cm (36in) wide
25 x 50cm (10 x 20in) cold-water soluble fabric
Pink and ivory sewing threads
Multicolour, silver and gold metallic machine embroidery threads
20cm (8in) embroidery hoop
Sewing thread for embroidering face
Assorted sewing threads for hair
Beading wire and fine steel wire
Polyester stuffing
Fine blunt screwdriver
Fine knitting needle
Hair-setting lotion
Pink nail varnish
Soft pink crayon
Wooden stand (optional)
Glue

To make up the doll

1 Enlarge doll outline to 125% and the clothes outlines to 156% and then to 128% using a photocopier (see pages 88–89). Cut out doll pattern pieces. Fold pink cotton fabric right sides together and draw upper body piece on to it. With machine set for set straight stitching, size 14/90 needle and pink sewing thread at top and bobbin, stitch layers together just inside line, leaving waist edges open (fig 1). Fold pink satin right sides together, draw around legs piece and repeat. Cut out body and legs pieces, snip into seam allowances at angles and curves, and turn through – pieces are small, so use a pin to ease turning.

2 Insert a length of beading wire from one hand across to other. Use fine steel wire to do the same for legs: if doll is to be mounted on a stand, wire in one leg should be pushed through toe to be glued into stand (fig 2).

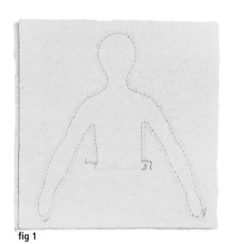

fig 1

fig 2

3 Using screwdriver as a packing tool, stuff body and legs firmly with polyester stuffing. Stitch across legs at ankles, knees and tops of thighs, and across arms at wrists, elbows and tops of arms. Join body and legs at waist, fold in cut edges to create a neat join and hand stitch together.

4 For a fuller face, cut a face piece (see below) from cotton fabric, fold cut edges under, stitch chin seam, fill with a little stuffing and stitch on to front of head with tiny hand slip stitches. Hand embroider a simple face and use soft pink crayon as rouge.

5 Make hair curls by twisting lengths of sewing thread around a fine knitting needle, and dampen with setting lotion. Allow to dry, remove ringlets and hand sew hair around head.

6 Paint on shoes using pink nail varnish. When varnish is dry, tie crossed threads around ankles and legs to simulate ballet slippers.

To make up the doll's clothes

1 Cut out a piece of net 25 x 6cm (10 x 2½in). From remaining net, cut out strips of veiling net 2.5cm (1in) wide. Set stitch length to 1, zigzag to 2 and, with ivory thread at top and bobbin, stitch along one long edge of a net strip, finger pleating to create a frill. Make 1m (1¼yd) of frill and cut into 4 equal lengths.

2 Lay unstitched edge of a frill along lower edge of net piece and stitch with straight stitch along zigzag line. Layer next frill to overlap first (fig 3), stitch, and repeat with remaining 2 frills to create a stiff petticoat. Fold short ends together and hand stitch into a tube, with frills on inside.

fig 3

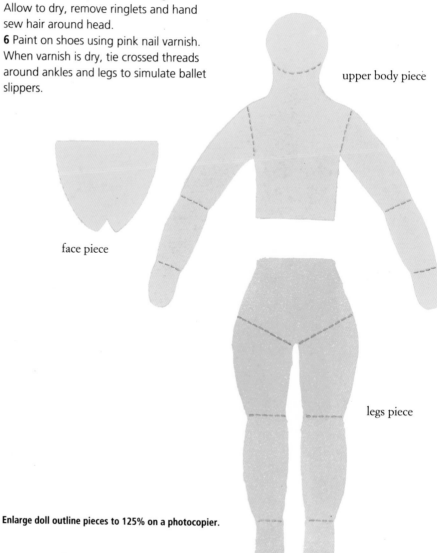

face piece

upper body piece

legs piece

Enlarge doll outline pieces to 125% on a photocopier.

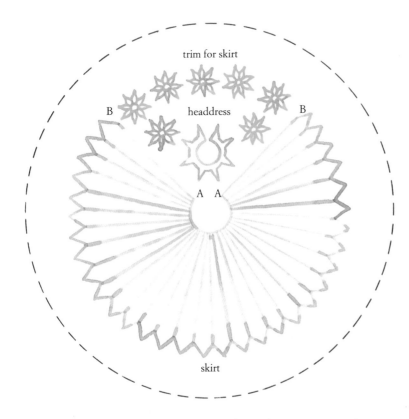

Enlarge clothes outlines to 156% and then to 128% on a photocopier.

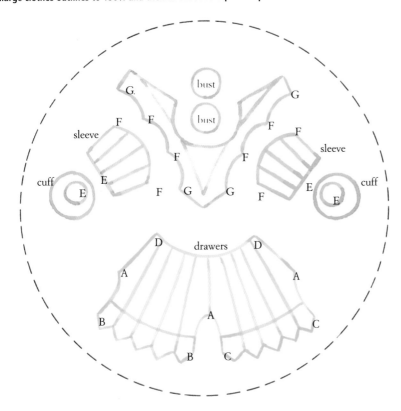

3 Remaining clothes are all stitched on soluble fabric stretched in an embroidery hoop. Lay hoop over enlarged circle pattern and trace skirt, head-dress and trim on to soluble fabric using a fine felt-tipped pen.

4 Remove presser foot, lower or cover teeth, insert 9/65 needle and thread top and bobbin with metallic threads: use either multicolour thread or silver thread at top and gold at bobbin. Stitch skirt outlines first, fill in with a mesh of stitching lines and stiffen edges with zigzag set to 2. Stitch flower trims with gold thread at top and bobbin, and head-dress with silver.

5 Trace remaining clothes outlines from enlarged pattern on to soluble fabric as before. For bodice, lay a piece of pink silk under hoop, right side to soluble fabric, with a piece of stiffening underneath. Using multicoloured metallic thread, stitch around 3 marked triangles and cut away excess fabric. Fill in all clothes pieces with a mesh of stitching lines as before, then stitch around neck edge of bodice with zigzag set to 2 and using silver thread. Finally, stitch around 3 triangles to give a boned, corset effect.

6 Check that lines of stitches are interlinked (see pages 80–81) and dissolve soluble fabric. While pieces are still damp, stretch 2 bust pieces over end of a pencil to create 2 domes. When dry, stuff with pieces of bodice silk. Sew drawers and bodice into clothes (refer to outlines for guide to joining seams).

7 Dress doll, securing clothes in place with tiny hand stitches. Drawers seam is in centre front; net skirt should dip down in front and flip up at back. Stitch on embroidered skirt so that net skirt is visible beneath. Put on bodice and hand stitch bust and cuffs on. Sew on crown. Finally, stitch on skirt rosettes.

8 Fix doll to wooden stand if desired.

evening wrap

Parallel rows of straight stitching create a geometric net to hold a shoal of bright silk snippings. The interlocking lines of thread create a surprisingly strong fabric, which can be used as an evening wrap or stole. Alternatively, by choosing different fabrics and thread colours, the technique could be used to make a sheer panel for a window.

Stitch methods

Set straight stitch
Set zigzag stitch
Tension: loosened bobbin tension throughout
Foot: normal presser foot
Needle: 12/80

You will need

For a wrap 200 x 44cm (78 x 17½in):
Assorted silk or fine fabrics, including narrow strips the length of finished wrap
200 x 88cm (78 x 35in) hot-water soluble fabric
2.5m (3yd) bonding web, 44cm (17½in) wide
2 large reels contrasting sewing threads

To work the net

1 Following manufacturer's instructions, back fabric pieces with bonding web. Remove paper backing, then cut out a mass of small shapes from fabric, either cutting around outlines printed on fabric or cutting out tiny scraps at random.
2 Cut out 2 pieces of soluble fabric, each 200 x 44cm (78 x 17½in). Lay fabric shapes over one piece of soluble fabric as shown in the photograph below left.
3 Using the iron at a very low heat setting, bond shapes to soluble fabric. Lay second piece of soluble fabric on top and pin the 2 layers together. Using a long ruler, draw a pencil line close to one long edge.
4 Thread top and bobbin with contrasting sewing threads. Loosen bobbin tension slightly so that bobbin colour appears on right side of fabric, set stitch length to 3 and stitch along pencil line in as straight a line as possible.
5 Stitch lines parallel to this, approximately 6mm (¼in) apart (use presser foot as a guide), all the way across fabric. Draw a second pencil line at right angles to first across width of soluble fabric, and stitch a second set of parallel lines in the same way.
6 Using a set square, draw a diagonal line across one corner (fig 1) and stitch a set of parallel, diagonal lines across fabric. Draw a diagonal line in opposite direction in adjoining corner and stitch a final set of parallel lines.
7 Remove soluble fabric following instructions on page 81. Dry and then press net.

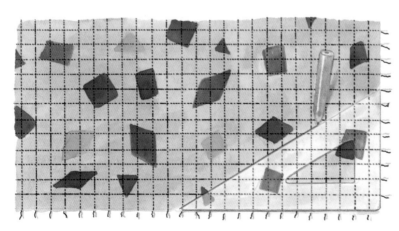

fig 1

fig 2

To work the border

1 Cut out 2 border strips of fabric, each 200cm (78in) long by 8cm (3in) wide, and 2 more border strips, each 44cm (17½in) long (the stole width) by 8cm (3in) wide. Back some other strips of fabric with bonding web and cut out 8 strips 200cm (78in) long, and 8 more strips 44cm (17½in) long, both sets being 8mm (⅜in) wide. Remove backing paper.
2 Fold all border strips in half lengthways, press, unfold and lay first backed fabric strip alongside crease of first border strip. Lay other strips alongside and press to bond (fig 2). Set stitch length to 1 and zigzag to 2.5, and sew over long cut edges with satin stitch.

Repeat for remaining 3 border strips.
3 When all strips have been stitched in position, fold border strips lengthways along pressed crease with wrong sides together. On appliquéd sides of border strips, trim cut edge outside last line of satin stitch. On other side, fold cut edge to wrong side so that back and front of border strip are the same width. Press.
4 Bind net edges with border strips. Work with right side of net and appliquéd side of strips up: net edges should be inside folded borders. Pin and tack 4 borders, then satin stitch along inner edges of border through net. Satin stitch border edges together at each corner (fig 3).

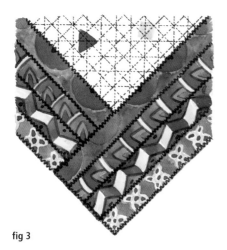

fig 3

91

tension effects

In the previous chapter we introduced the idea of using a loosened top tension to create a speckled texture and colouring in machine embroidery. The tension effects described below are created with a loosened bobbin tension and are much more exaggerated, creating exuberant stitching which can be worked to resemble hand embroidery, combined with other fabric decoration such as appliqué, or stitched in swirling lines or spirals to create glorious abstract patterns.

Using loosened bobbin tension

For anyone who has been taught sewing or has dutifully digested their sewing-machine manual, the first few stitches with a dramatically loosened bobbin tension can be quite a shock: instead of an even line of stitches, loops of the bobbin thread will be scattered across the fabric. But persevere – what may initially look like a mistake can be refined into a variety of distinct and delightful stitch effects.

Practise the different stitches below to discover the extent of your machine's capabilities: there will come a point when the tension difference will be too great and one thread will continually snap. Then use the different effects selectively to add a joyful abandon to more sedate projects.

Setting up the machine

Set up the machine for free stitching, with teeth lowered or covered, stitch length set at 0 and no foot, but remember to lower the presser bar. Use a slightly thicker needle than normal: 14/90 or 16/100.

Start with the zigzag width set at 0, but then experiment with different widths. For first experiments, fit the fabric in an embroidery hoop and use different colours of top and bobbin thread so that it is quite obvious which thread is which.

Tension

Individual adjustments will be described for each effect, but it is important to remember two points:
• There must be some tension for the machine to work properly: if both top and bobbin are completely loose, the threads will simply disappear into the shuttle race and break.

• Although the two tensions are adjusted separately, altering one always affects the other. If one is loosened, the effect will be enhanced by tightening the other, and if one is tightened and the other is not loosened, the tightened thread will try to pull the other through the fabric, but because there is no give the thread being pulled is likely to break.

Starting to stitch

Whip stitch   **Feather stitch**

Whip stitch

If the bobbin tension is loosened and the top tension tightened, the top thread will lie on the fabric surface and the bobbin thread will whip around it.

Practise stitching at different speeds and moving the hoop more and less quickly to create different lengths of stitch. Stitching on the spot with a loosened bobbin tension can create decorative knots but is wearing on the top thread, which may break.

Feather stitch

Feather stitch is an exaggerated version of whip stitch, achieved with a very loose bobbin tension and tight top tension. Stitch quickly to create the distinctive loops on the fabric surface.

This stitch is best worked in whirls or circles, as straight lines tend to unravel. If lines are desired, after stitching paint the wrong side with a PVA-based craft glue, or iron a strip of iron-on interfacing over the back of the stitches.

Cording

Cording

With the tensions set for whip stitch, practise working very small stitches so that the bobbin thread completely wraps the top thread, creating a corded effect.

It may help to loosen the bobbin tension further or to tighten the top tension; the effect can be increased by using a heavier top thread, which will automatically tighten the top tension.

Cable stitch

Cable stitch can resemble cording, but is worked in reverse: the bobbin is wound with thick thread and the tension settings are altered to create a loosened top tension and slightly tightened bobbin tension, so that the bobbin thread remains below the surface and the top thread is pulled down to wrap around it. The fabric is stitched with the wrong side up, so that when it is turned over the thicker bobbin thread is lying on the surface of the right side.

Quite thick threads, including knitting and embroidery cottons, can be wound around the bobbin by hand. Avoid any fluffy or bobbly threads, but otherwise, if it will pull through the delivery eye on the case, it should stitch.

Do experiment: using a heavy bobbin thread may be enough on its own to pull the top thread down. Once a satisfactory effect has been perfected, try using looser top tensions to create a feather stitch, or loosen the bobbin tension further to allow the bobbin thread to twist on the lower surface.

Loose zigzag

Working zigzag stitch with a loose bobbin tension and tight top tension can create a variety of effects.

If the bobbin tension is loosened slightly and the top tightened slightly, the effect will be a bicoloured, fairly flat stitch. If the bobbin tension is quite loose and the top tension tight, the distinct zigzag will disappear, and instead the bobbin thread will form uneven horizontal straight stitches and the top thread will appear as a slightly meandering line in the centre.

Loose tailor tacking

Using a tailor-tacking foot (which automatically creates a line of loops) with a loosened bobbin tension and tightened top tension will create an extravagant mass of loops. The stitches are so loose that it is quite easy to pull out the top thread gently and leave two distinct rows of loops.

Whether the top thread is in or out, the stitches are quite vulnerable. Either fix them on the wrong side by painting with a PVA-based glue or ironing on a strip of iron-on interfacing, or trap them under a bonded layer of organza (see pages 94–96).

Problem solving

• Breaking threads are the most common problem, and are usually caused by one tension being tightened without the other being loosened.
• Using different weights of thread may cause problems – try a larger needle for the top thread. Heavy bobbin threads in a loosened bobbin case may cause the screw to work its way out. If so, replace it immediately.
• When using unusual threads, listen carefully to the machine. If it sounds laboured or makes a clunk, stop and investigate. Most problems are likely to be caused by fluff in the bobbin shuttle or a loose thread catching, but trying to force the stitching will pull the shuttle race out of alignment.

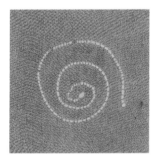

Cable stitch

Loose zigzag

Loose tailor tacking

table settings

One of the great advantages of machine embroidery is that although some of the effects can look quite ethereal, the machine stitching means that it is actually very strong, so if you choose washable fabrics and use mercerized threads the finished items will be relatively hardwearing despite their delicate appearance. This final project uses a combination of tension techniques and shadow effects to create table settings for the seriously stylish. The embroidered effects were worked without an embroidery hoop, but for less experienced stitchers a hoop might be a help.

Stitch methods
Set straight stitch
Free straight stitch
Free satin stitch
Tension: normal and loosened bobbin tension
Feet: tailor-tacking foot; normal presser foot for making up
Needle: 12/90

You will need
For 4 napkins and rings:
4 different-coloured pieces lightweight cotton fabric, each 15 x 25cm (6 x 10in)
4 pieces contrast-coloured organzas, each 15 x 25cm (6 x 10in)

50 x 30cm (20 x 12in) iron-on bonding web
Silk, velvet and satin scraps
1m (1¼yd) square plain fabric, for napkins
20 x 18cm (8 x 7in) lining fabric, for rings
Sewing threads in assorted colours, including napkin colour
Thicker bobbin thread
Monofilament nylon thread
PVA-based craft glue
For 1 table mat:
50 x 35cm (20 x 14in) each coloured cotton fabric, contrasting organza, iron-on bonding web, lining fabric
Silk, velvet and satin scraps
Assorted sewing threads
Thicker bobbin thread
50 x 35cm (20 x 14in) paper

Layering and embroidering the fabric
The fabric for the outside of napkin rings, the appliqué on the napkins and the mat is formed in the same way and then made up into individual items. Contrasting scraps are trapped between the base cotton fabric and organza, and embroidery can be worked both on base cotton and over the organza, creating a mulitcoloured, layered fabric.
1 Stitch some random lines of embroidery on coloured cotton fabric, using a selection of tension effects described on pages 92–93.
2 Lay embroidered fabric on a flat surface for ironing: use an ironing board for small pieces, place several layers of towel or blanket on a table for larger ones.
3 Cut out tiny scraps of fabric to trap. Scraps can be laid on cotton and under bonding web, and will be seen under

the layer of organza, or can be laid on bonding web and will initially be under organza, but organza can then be cut away to reveal true colour of fabric scrap. Lay down some scraps, reserving any in velvet or with raised effects for revealing later.

4 Remove paper backing from bonding web and lay it over the cotton. Lay more scraps of fabric on web, lay down random lengths of coloured cotton thread if desired, lay organza on top and bond by ironing. Melting of adhesive web will bond fabrics tightly together and may cause a slight marbling or graduation of colour.

5 Using sharp embroidery scissors, cut away organza above second layer of scraps (on top of bonding web). Cut edges can be left, or outlined with a loosened zigzag.

6 Stitch more random lines of embroidery over organza, using tension effects described on pages 92–93.

To make up a napkin ring

1 Cut out a strip of layered fabric 18.5 x 5.5cm (7¼ x 2¼ in). Fold 5mm (¼ in) to wrong side on 1 short and 2 long edges and press.

2 Cut out a strip of lining 18 x 5cm (7 x 2in) and a strip of bonding web 17 x 4cm (6½ x 1½ in). Lay bonding web in centre of wrong side of lining, iron it to bond, remove backing paper and fold 5mm (¼ in) overlap of lining over bonding web along all edges.

3 With bonding web down, lay lining strip on wrong side of layered strip, with short folded-over ends even and lining central on layered strip along length

fig 1

fig 2

(fig 1). Iron to bond. Thread machine with monofilament thread at top and bobbin, adjust for set stitching and stitch along lining edge from uneven end to 5mm (¼ in) from even ends, across strip, back along other edge and finally across to start of stitching.

4 Following manufacturer's instructions, apply craft glue carefully and sparingly to both sides of unfolded end of layered fabric and insert between lining and layered fabric to form a ring (fig 2). Hold together tightly until glued.

To make up the napkins

1 Cut out napkin fabric into 4 even squares. Fold over a narrow double hem around each square, thread machine with thread to match napkin fabric at top and in bobbin, and stitch with straight stitch.

2 From remnants of layered fabric used for napkin rings, cut out 4 6.5cm (2½ in) squares and on each cut a gentle curve from opposite corners to make a quarter circle shape.

3 Appliqué a quarter circle at the corner of each napkin, using set zigzag stitch.

To make up a mat

1 Fold paper rectangle into quarters and cut away a gentle curve at free corners to make a pleasing oval.

2 Use this pattern to cut out a layered oval and a lining oval.

3 With right sides together, lay ovals one on the other and sew all round with a 1.5cm (⅝ in) seam allowance, leaving a gap for turning. Trim and clip notches into seam allowance all round, turn and press. Slip stitch gap closed by hand.

Motifs & stitch samplers

On the following pages you will find a selection of alternative designs or motifs for some of the projects in the book. These include a selection of quilting outlines; two stitching samplers, which provide suitable outlines for practising free-stitching techniques; two alphabets, one with upright letters, both large and small, ideal for initials or bold lettering and a second more flowing one with letters suitable for monograms, names or messages; a superb spread of motifs for the Pieced Tablecloth; and alternative designs for the Button Collection and Pins with Panache.

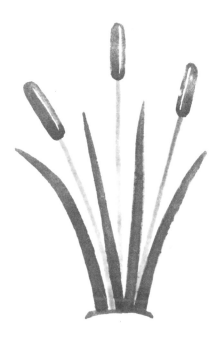

quilting motifs

See Summer, Winter Bedspread on page 40

The top quilt on pages 40–41 is quilted by stitching around the printed flowers on the fabric, but not all fabrics are printed with such suitable outlines. If you would rather quilt a plain fabric, a tiny check or an all-over pattern, choose one of the outline shapes shown here. Enlarge to the required size using a photocopier, and transfer the full-size outline on to card to use as a template. Draw around the template on to the fabric using a vanishing pen or a sharp, hard pencil to create an outline around which to quilt. If you are not sure how many outlines to draw, use the template to cut out a number of paper shapes and lay them on the quilt to create a pleasing design.

straight-stitch sampler

The outlines given here are intended for practising the free machine-embroidery techniques with a darning foot described on pages 44–45 and the embroidery techniques without a foot on pages 50–51. The four designs in the corners are intended as stitching suggestions only and there is no need to transfer them on to fabric – just try to reproduce them with stitching. The geometric or pictorial motif outlines could be transferred (see pages 18–19) and then filled with stitches. Either work the motifs on scraps of fabric, or work them all on a piece of calico to form a sampler.

satin-stitch sampler

The stitching suggestions and outlines here are intended for practising free-stitching techniques using zigzag and satin-stitch settings, as described on page 60. The four corner designs are stitching suggestions to practise and perhaps use as filling techniques for large areas. When working satin-stitch daisies or beads of colour, remember that the needle only swings from side to side, so to create petals radiating all around a centre or beads lying at different angles the fabric must be moved.

alphabets

See Pieced Tablecloth on page 74

The lettering used on the Pieced Tablecloth on pages 74–79 is the designer's own handwriting, written large. If you wish to embroider the words on the tablecloth, romantic messages on a pillowcase, names on laundry bags or other words, either write them yourself or use the flowing script provided here (below). To use the lower script for the tablecloth, enlarge it to the required size on a photocopier. The top alphabet with the fine letters would be easy to work in couching (see page 72) or either of the straight-stitch methods described on page 73; the lower, more flowing, italic-like script would be better worked with one of the satin-stitch methods on page 73.

ABCDE
MNOP
WXYZ

mnopqrst

ABCDEFGH
RSTUVWXYZ
pqrstuvwxyz 123

F G H I J K L
Q Q R S T U V
a b c d e f g h i j k l
u v w x y z ～

I J K L M N O P Q
a b c d e f g h i j k l m n o
3 4 4 5 6 6 7 8 8 9 0

tools of the trade

See Pieced Tablecloth on page 74

The Pieced Tablecloth on pages 74–79 is covered with wonderful fishy dishes, but it could just as well be embroidered with a selection of other designs. A striking alternative to food but with similar gastronomic appeal would be a selection of kitchen implements. You could use some of these motifs to embroider a tea cosy, the back of oven gloves, a shelf edging or cushions. Enlarge the motifs if necessary, using a photocopier.

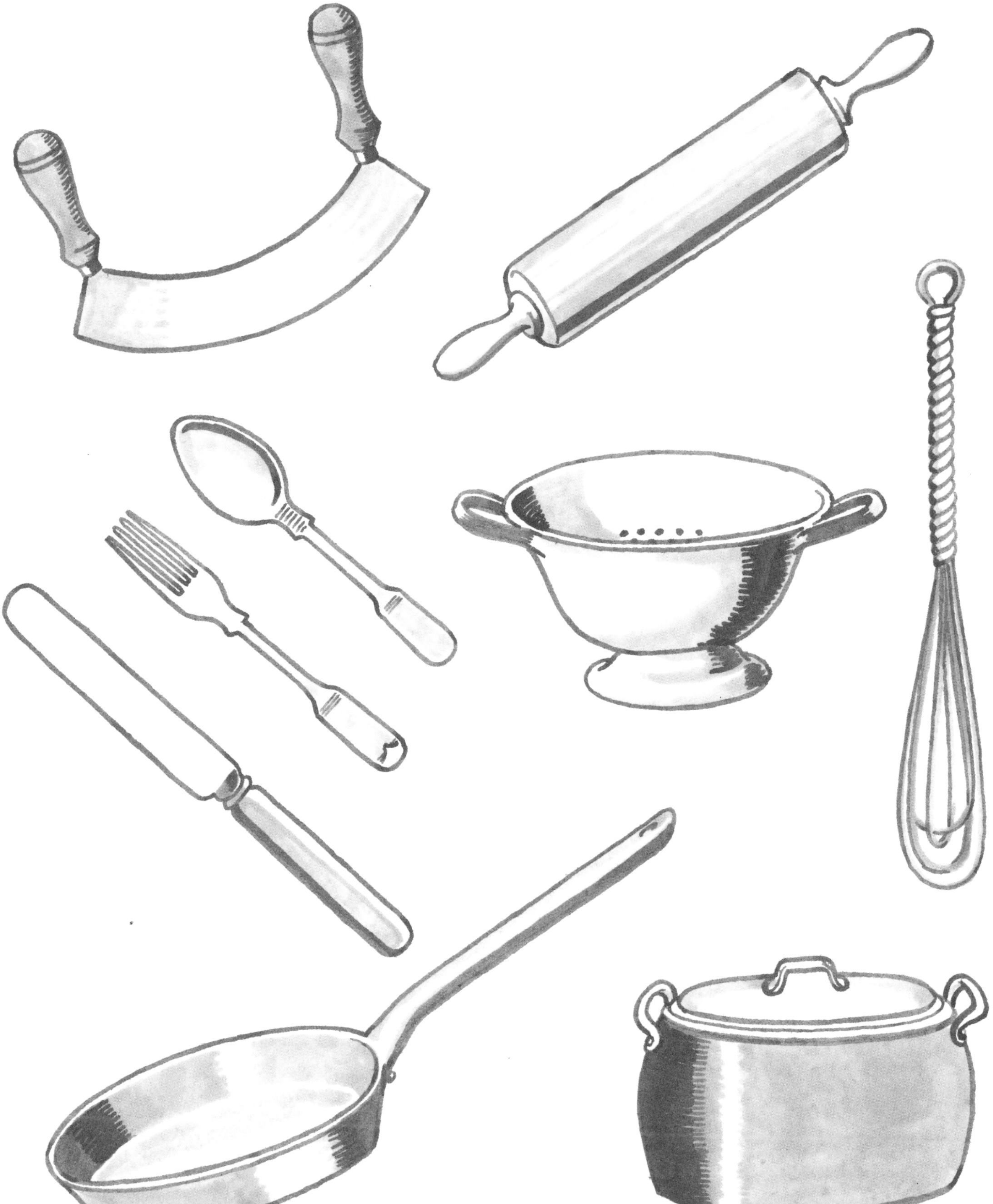

button &
brooch
alternatives

See Button Collection on page 62 and
Pins with Panache on page 82

The stars, flowers or simple stripes shown
here would all be suitable designs to use
as alternatives to the heart designs on the
buttons in the collection on pages 62–63;
to use on 29mm (1⅛in) buttons, reduce to
64% on a photocopier. Alternatively, use
any of the round designs for brooches
worked on vanishing muslin, following
the instructions for Pins with Panache
on pages 82–85. There are also three
alternative pin designs. The dots around
the designs on the right indicate the
position for beads and are not intended
to be stitched.

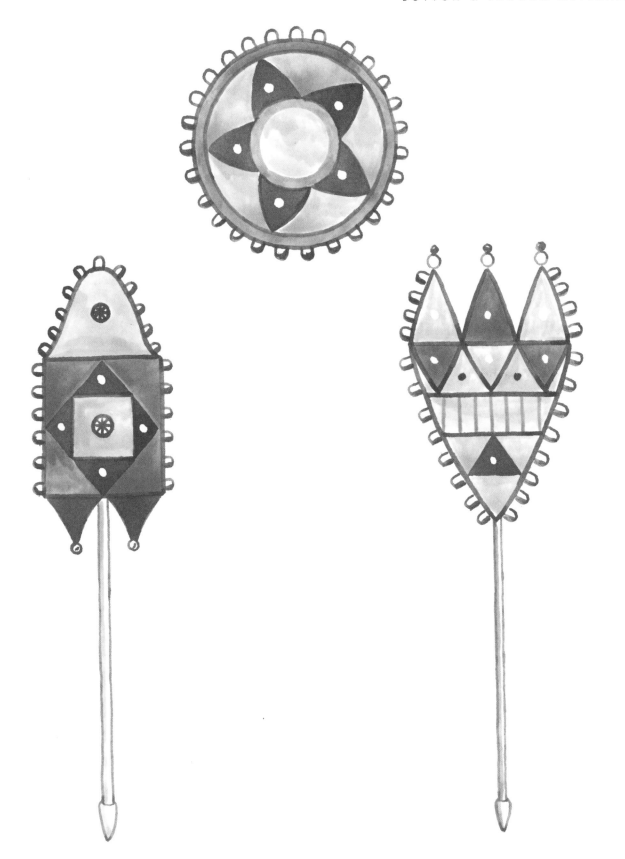

index

acknowledgments

The author would like to thank all those who made the writing of this book possible: Gabi Tubbs for her vision, Jane O'Shea for her warm support and guidance, Vanessa Courtier for her sense of style, Kate Simunek for her delightful illustrations, Linda Burgess for her inspired photography, Sarah Widdicombe and Patsy North for their sensitive and meticulous editing and Kathy Seely for her unfailing help.

Particular thanks to the needlewomen in my family: Rosemary Bennett, Elsa Wheatcroft and Elizabeth Hook who inspired and taught me the pleasure of making and stitching; to my two small daughters, Hester and Beatrix for their enthusiasm and to my husband Rob, for his encouragement.

The author and publisher would like to thank the textile artists who designed and made the projects and without whom the book would have remained unwritten: Marie Wahed (Bags of Style), Helen Ashworth (Crib Cover and Summer, Winter Bedspread), Diana Mott-Thornton (Pleated & Pressed Cushions and Evening Wrap), Karen Howse (Decorated Box), Rosalind Brown (Silk Lampshade), Helen Banzhaf (Book Binder), Claire Sowden (Button Collection), Linda Miller (Lying on a Rug), Sarah Denison (Pieced Tablecloth), Janice Gilmore (Pins with Panache), Louise Brownlow (Dancing Doll) and Kate Peacock (Table Settings).

Special thanks to Judy Barry, Senior Lecturer, Embroidery Course, Department of Textiles and Fashion, Manchester Metropolitan University and Course Tutor, Department of Textiles and Fashion, Royal College of Art, for her invaluable advice and technical expertise. Many thanks to Madeira for their help and selection of threads.

The publisher thanks Ian Muggeridge for D.T.P. assistance.